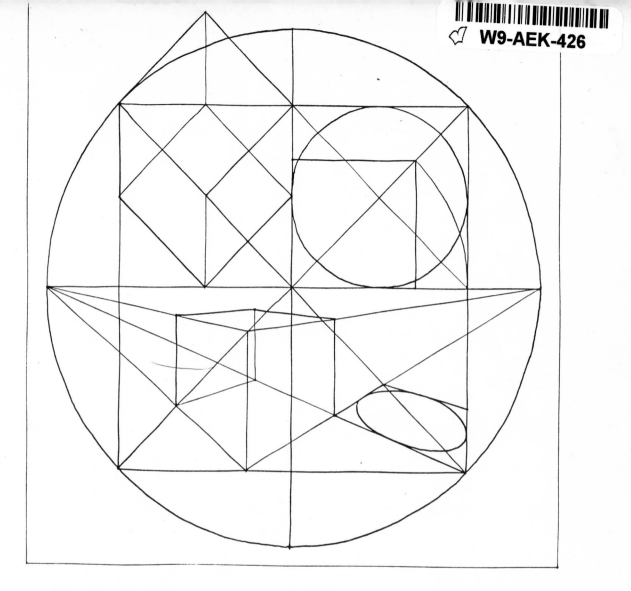

ARCHITECTURAL
GRAPHICS

FRANK CHING

VNR VAN NOSTRAND REINHOLD COMPANY

NEW YORK · CINCINNATI · TORONTO · LONDON · MELBOURNE

dedicated to my mother and father...

Van Nostrand Reinhold Company Regional Offices
New York   Cincinnati   Chicago   Millbrae   Dallas

Van Nostrand Reinhold Company International Offices
London   Toronto   Melbourne

Copyright © 1975 by Litton Educational Publishing, Inc.
Library of Congress Catalog Card No. 74-15248
ISBN 0-442-21531-2 paper ISBN 0-442-21530-4

Designed by Frank Ching

Published by Van Nostrand Reinhold Company
A Division of Litton Educational Publishing, Inc.

16 15 14 13 12 11 10 9 8 7

Library of Congress Cataloging in Publication Data

Ching, Frank, 1943-
    Architectural Graphics.

    Includes index.
    1. Architectural drawing.   I. Title
NA2700.C46   720'.28   74-15248

TABLE OF CONTENTS

FOREWORD

The purpose of this primer is to acquaint the beginning student with the range of graphic tools which are available for conveying architectural ideas. The basic premise behind its formulation is that graphics is an inseparable part of the design process, an important tool which provides the designer with the means not only of presenting a design proposal but also of communicating with himself and others in the design studio.

It is important to note here that graphic communication requires mental skill as well as manual skill. We must recognize that graphics, the physical end product we are always concerned with, is itself the result of a design process, a careful analysis of why, when, and where a graphic technique is employed, as well as the execution of a technique.

The various graphic conventions and techniques are presented and the rationale behind their use is explained. The order of the chapters does not imply a specific sequence to the coverage of the material, but rather, it attempts to structure the field of architectural graphics into a comprehensible format.

This handbook is not intended to be a primer on design or a handbook on sophisticated rendering techniques. No definitive drawing style is emphasized or encouraged. Each of us inevitably develops his or her own style of drawing through practice and experience.

EQUIPMENT & MATERIALS

Although your own hand and mind control the finished drawing, quality equipment and materials make drawing a more enjoyable experience, and the achievement of quality work becomes much easier in the long run.

DRAWING PENCILS

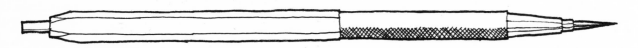

This is the traditional leadholder. Due to its relatively thick lead it is capable of a variety of sharp line weights. The beginner should practice sharpening the point until he develops the ability to rotate the pencil sufficiently while drawing (see page 18).

This mechanical pencil utilizes a .5 mm lead, which does not require sharpening. It is capable of consistently sharp, fine lines if you rotate it sufficiently while drawing. For relatively thick, bold lines you have to use a series of lines.

The common wood/lead pencil can also be used for drafting. The wood must be shaved back to expose 3/4" of the lead shaft so that it can be sharpened like the leadholder.

All three types of pencils are capable of producing quality drawings. Your preference is a matter of choice and your particular skills.

RECOMMENDED LEAD WEIGHTS:

The degree of hardness of a drawing lead is dependent on:

① the grade of lead, which ranges from 9H (extremely hard) to 6B (extremely soft)

② paper type and finish (degree of tooth or roughness): the more tooth a paper has, the harder the lead you should use

③ the drawing surface: the harder the surface, the softer the lead feels

④ humidity: high humidity conditions tend to increase the apparent hardness of the lead

4H
- hard and dense
- for accurate layouts
- not for finished drawings
- do not use with a heavy hand; grooves drawing paper and may not erase easily
- doesn't print well

2H
- medium-hard
- hardest grade feasible for finished drawings
- doesn't erase easily if used heavily

F and H
- medium
- excellent general-purpose lead weight
- for layouts, finished drawings, and lettering

HB
LETTERING
- soft
- for dense, bold linework and lettering
- requires control for fine linework
- erases easily
- prints well
- tends to smear easily

borders

The technical pen, capable of precise line widths, can be used for both freehand and drafted ink drawings. As with leadholders, technical pens vary somewhat in form and operation, depending on the manufacturer. Most technical pens, however, utilize an ink-flow-regulating wire within a tubular point, the size of which determines the finished ink-line width. There are a dozen point sizes available, from 5X0 (extremely fine) to 6 (2mm).

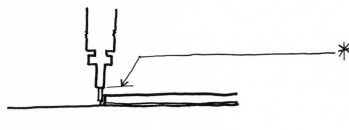

3 X 0	.1 mm
2 X 0	.2 mm
1	.4 mm
3	.8 mm

A starting pen set should include the point sizes indicated on the left.

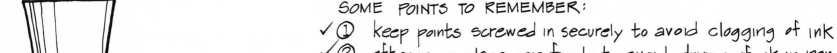

* Make sure that the pen you use has a point tube that is long enough to clear the thickness of your triangles and straightedge.

SOME POINTS TO REMEMBER:

✓① keep points screwed in securely to avoid clogging of ink
✓② after use replace cap firmly to avoid drying of ink in pen
✓③ when not in use store pens with their points up

DRAWING INK
BLACK

Use waterproof, black drawing ink. Pelican Fount India is a good nonclogging ink specially formulated for use in fountain pens but also suitable for technical pens.

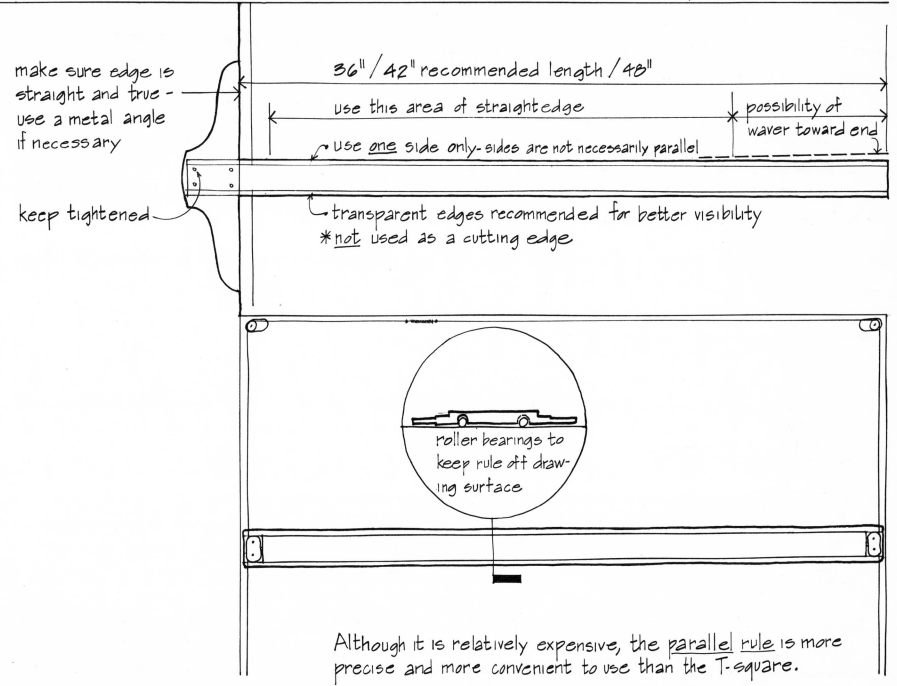

make sure edge is straight and true - use a metal angle if necessary

36" / 42" recommended length / 48"

use this area of straightedge

possibility of waver toward end

use one side only - sides are not necessarily parallel

keep tightened

transparent edges recommended for better visibility
* not used as a cutting edge

roller bearings to keep rule off drawing surface

Although it is relatively expensive, the parallel rule is more precise and more convenient to use than the T-square.

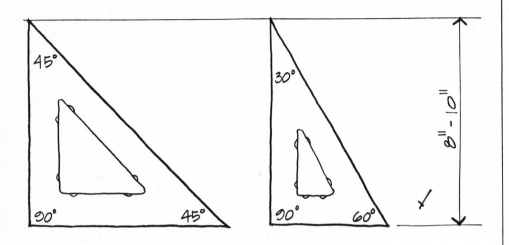

45°   90°   45°

30°   90°   60°

8" – 10"

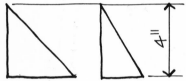

4"

small triangles are useful for crosshatching of small areas and hand lettering (see page 106)

the adjustable triangle is useful for drawing sloping lines of stairs, pitched roofs, etc.

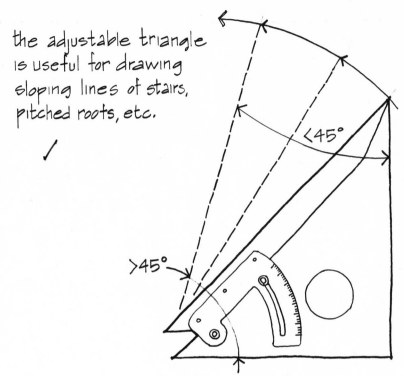

<45°

>45°

the 45°·45° and 30°·60° triangles can be used in combination to produce increments of 15°

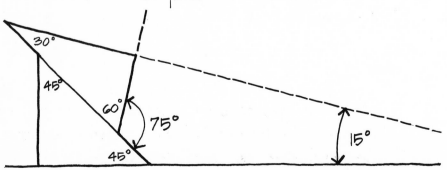

30°

45°

60°   75°

45°

15°

QUALITY CHARACTERISTICS

- acrylic / nonyellowing
- scratch-resistant
- ease of readability
- good edge retention
- finger lifts

- <u>don't</u> use as a cutting edge

- <u>don't</u> use with Magic Markers

- <u>do</u> keep clean with a mild cleanser or lighter fluid

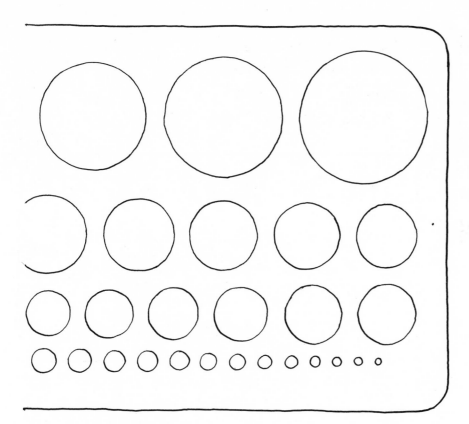

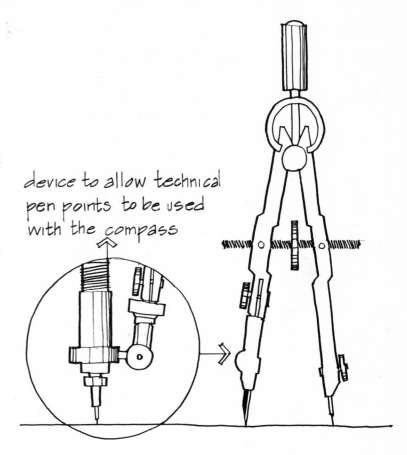

device to allow technical
pen points to be used
with the compass

the circle template is a time-saving device
useful for small circles of even radii

other useful templates include
geometric shapes, plumbing fixtures, and furnishings

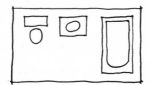

for curves of uneven radii use
a french curve

the compass is useful for circles of inde-
terminate radii, large circles, and most
ink work

care must be taken to match line weights of
circles to the rest of the drawing, whether
in pencil or in ink (see page 19)

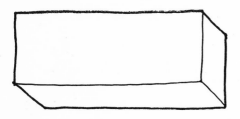

always use the softest
eraser compatible with
the job to avoid marring
the drawing surface

recommended brands:

Pink Pearl	Eberhard Faber
Magic Rub	Faber-Castell
Mars Plastic	Mars Staedtler

avoid use of ink erasers,
which are generally too
abrasive for drawing sur-
faces

erasing shield: use one
with square holes
enables you to erase pre-
cise areas of a drawing -
also useful to protect
drawing surface while
using an electric eraser

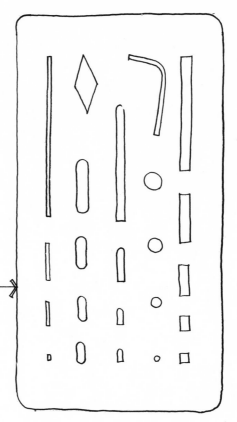

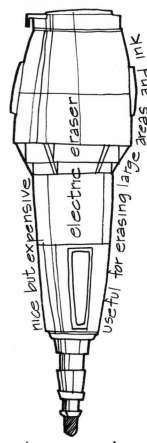

electric eraser

nice but expensive

useful for erasing large areas and ink

Use Pounce powder to prepare drawing surfaces
before inking.

drafting brush to keep
drawing surface clean

Skum-X is a soft, granular material that provides a temporary protective coating over
pencil drawings during drafting. If used too
heavily, it can cause lines to skip, so use
sparingly.

DESIRABLE CHARACTERISTICS:

• precision calibrated graduations
• engraved markings
• warp-resistant

* <u>not</u> to be used as a straight edge!

• triangular: 6 sides
11 scales

• flat-beveled: 8 scales

• flat-beveled: 8 scales

ARCHITECT'S SCALES: 1/8" = 1' 0 3/16" = 1' 0 3/8" = 1' 0 1/2" = 1' 0 1 1/2" = 1' 0 1/16" = 1' 0
         1/4" = 1' 0 3/32" = 1' 0 3/4" = 1' 0 1" = 1' 0 3" = 1' 0

ENGINEER'S SCALES: 10/20/30/40/50/60 parts to the inch

METRIC SCALES: 1:100 1:125 1:200 1:250 1:500 1:750 1:1000

TRACING PAPERS/ILLUSTRATION BOARDS/DRAWING SURFACES

Tracing papers are characterized by transparency, whiteness, and tooth. Slick papers are generally better for inking, while some degree of tooth is necessary for pencilwork.

① sketch-grade	② medium-grade	③ quality grade	④ film
• lightweight tissue • inexpensive • for sketching, doodling, quick overlays	• medium-weight/16-lb. • fine or medium tooth • for general layouts, preliminaries	• vellum/16- or 20-lb. • 100 percent rag • for finished drawings	• .004" clear polyester film for clearest reproductions, permanence, and overlays
• Dietzgen 161 Y • Charette 903	• Winston • Charette Bond • Boston Bond	• Bruning 500 • Clearprint 1000 H • Charprint 920 H	• Dupont Mylar • Arkwright • Herculene

Illustration boards are used for finished presentations. 100 percent-rag boards, medium weight or heavyweight, are recommended. Strathmore illustration boards are more dense than others and white clear through, making them useful for architectural models. Cold press illustration boards have more tooth than hot press boards, which have relatively smooth surfaces.

The following are used to cover drawing boards:
① vinyl covers provide a smooth, even drawing surface - tack holes and cuts heal themselves
② plastic-coated paper with a formica surface
③ a white, <u>dense</u> illustration board is an inexpensive drawing surface

ARCHITECTURAL DRAFTING

The basis for most architectural drawing is the line, and <u>the essence of a line is its continuity</u>. In a pure-line drawing, the architectural information conveyed (volumetric space; definition of planar elements, solids and voids; depth) depends primarily on the visual weight of the line types used and their discernible differences.

LINE WEIGHTS / LINE TYPES

LINE WEIGHTS: _____ major/primary • cuts/profiles/slices through spaces

HB   F/H

_____ secondary • elevations/corners/intersections of planes

HB   F/H

_____ grid/layout/rendition • construction/layout/lines on planes/textures

F/H   2H   4H

LINE TYPES: _____ solid/cut/profile lines
_____ solid/elevational lines
— — — — — — — dash lines/elements above cut
- - - - - - - - - - dash lines/elements below cut
note proportion between dashes and spaces between them
(—|‖—): keep tight for better line continuity

___ · ___ · ___ centerlines: longer lines should be approximately equal

grid lines/grid of centerlines
generally used to indicate a modular or structural system

___ - - ___ - - ___ boundary or property lines

___ - - - ___ - - - ___ lines of communication
—G——S——W— utility lines

<u>line quality</u> refers to <u>sharpness and clarity</u>,
<u>blackness</u>, and
<u>appropriate weight</u>

While inked lines vary only in width (unless their value is diluted), pencil lines can vary in both value and width. Thus, a pencil line's weight is controlled by the density of the lead used (affected by grade of lead, drawing surface, humidity) as well as the pressure with which you draw.

It is essential that you understand as you draw what each line represents, whether it is an edge, an intersection of two planes, or simply a change in material or texture.

<u>All lines should start and end definitely</u>, always touching at their ends, always bearing a logical relationship to other lines from beginning to end.

lines which fade out become arbitrary _____

a slight exaggeration at the ends helps to fix a line _____

when corners are not met crisply, they appear rounded

correct

single-stroke lines are always preferable

excessive overlap at corners appears out of proportion to size of drawing

<u>Corners are critical.</u> All lines should touch one another <u>crisply</u> at all corners.

17

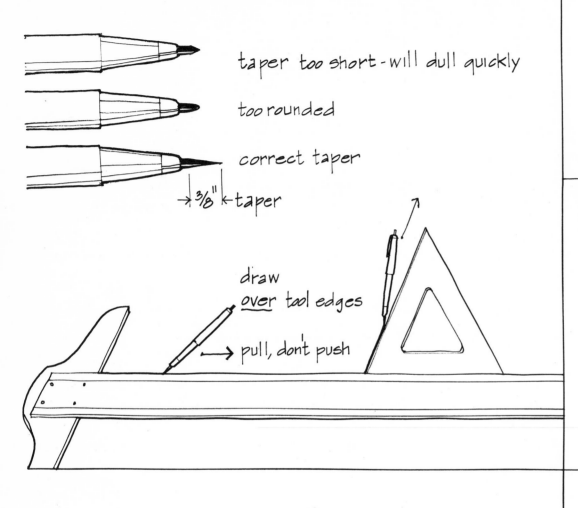

taper too short - will dull quickly

too rounded

correct taper

→ ⅜" ← taper

if you use sandpaper to sharpen leads, slant them at a low angle to achieve the correct taper

there are some excellent mechanical sharpeners available

draw over tool edges

→ pull, don't push

do not draw into corners - dirties equipment and causes blotting

rotate pencil while drawing

45° - 60°

draw over straightedge, leaving a very slight gap between the straightedge and lead or pen-point

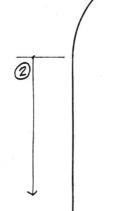

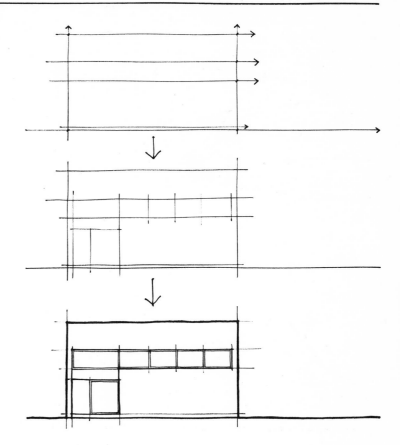

① ②

← to avoid noticeably mismatched tangents, always draw circular segments first, then draw straight-line segments from the curved lines

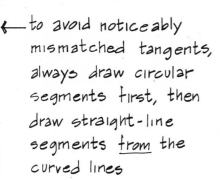

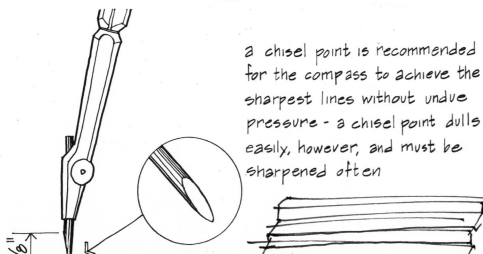

a chisel point is recommended for the compass to achieve the sharpest lines without undue pressure - a chisel point dulls easily, however, and must be sharpened often

3/8"

the order in which you should layout a drawing is:

① lightly block out the major horizontal and vertical lines
② fill in the secondary lines
③ heavy up the final lines, keeping in mind the proper line weight of each line

do not scrub your lines in; strive for single-stroke lines

ARCHITECTURAL DRAWING CONVENTIONS

The following section is concerned with the principal conventions of architectural drawing, their intentions, their capabilities, and their use in architectural graphics. They are considered here in terms of pure-line drawings. The rendition of values and context is discussed in chapter 4.

Plan/section/elevation views are the primary architectural drawings. They are orthographic in nature: the observer's line of sight is perpendicular to both the drawing plane and the principal surfaces of the building viewed. Conversely, the drawing surface is parallel to the major surfaces of the building.

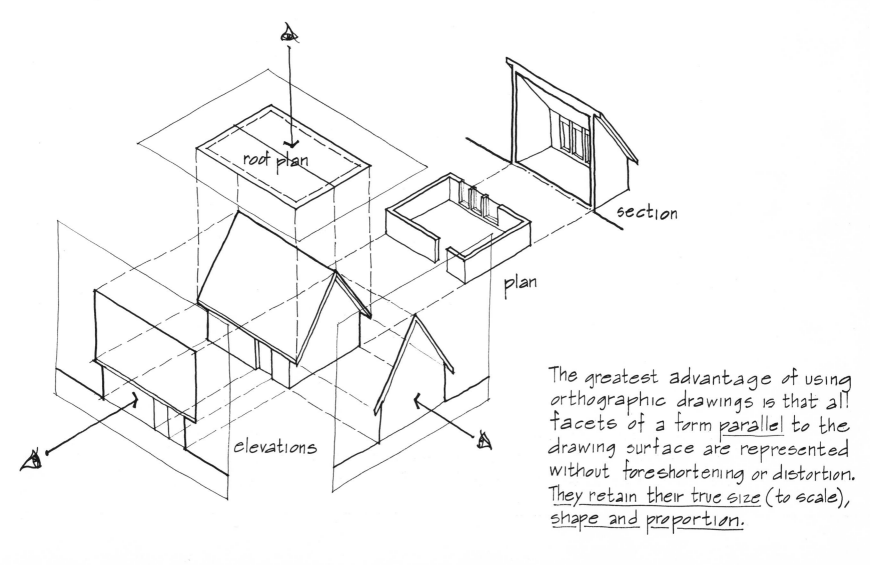

roof plan

section

plan

elevations

The greatest advantage of using orthographic drawings is that all facets of a form parallel to the drawing surface are represented without foreshortening or distortion. They retain their true size (to scale), shape and proportion.

In using plan/section/elevation drawings to represent architecture, we are in fact utilizing an __abstract__ method to represent reality.

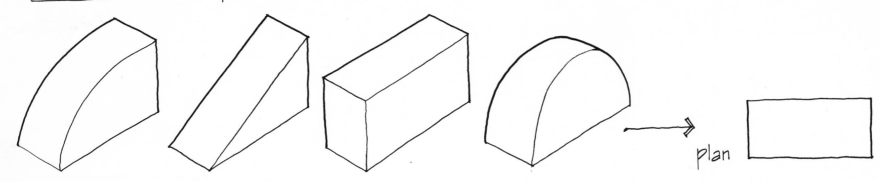

plan

Although these four objects have different forms, the __plan__ views for all of them (looking straight down are __identical__. Because of this the relationship between plan, section, and elevation views is critical for the description and comprehension of what we are drawing. When utilizing plan, section, and elevation drawings to describe architecture, we must see them as __a series of related views__, all of which contribute to the understanding of what we are drawing.

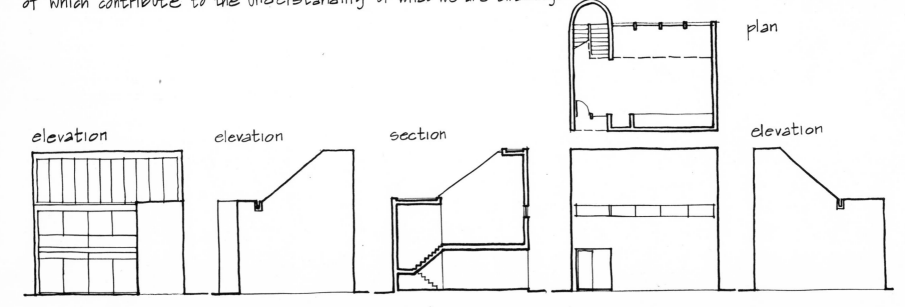

plan

elevation   elevation   section   elevation

The _floor plan_ and the _building section_ (see pages 30-31) are both sections or cuts: the plan is cut horizontally; the building section, vertically. Whereas in working drawings (for the purpose of construction) plans and sections show the way buildings are put together, in design and presentation drawings the primary purpose of floor plans and building sections is to illustrate the forms and relationships of positive and negative spaces, and the nature of defining elements and surfaces.

The floor plan is a sectional view looking down after a horizontal plane has been cut through a building and the top section removed.

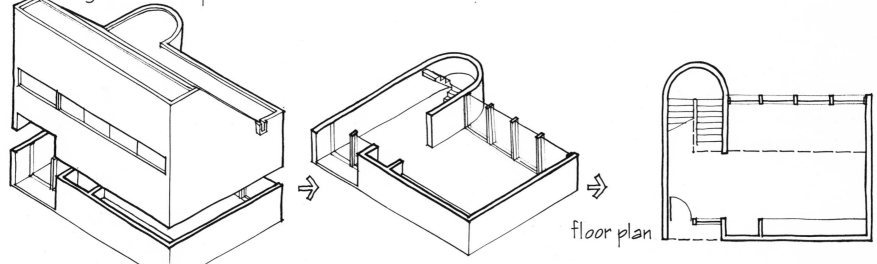

floor plan

The horizontal section is generally cut through all major vertical elements and all door and window openings. Usually this cut is about 4' above the floor, but this can vary slightly, depending on what you want to illustrate.

Floor plans are normally drawn at a scale of 1/8"=1'0 or 1/4"=1'0, but for large buildings and complexes the scale can be smaller. The larger the scale of the floor plan, the more detail has to be shown to give the drawing credibility.

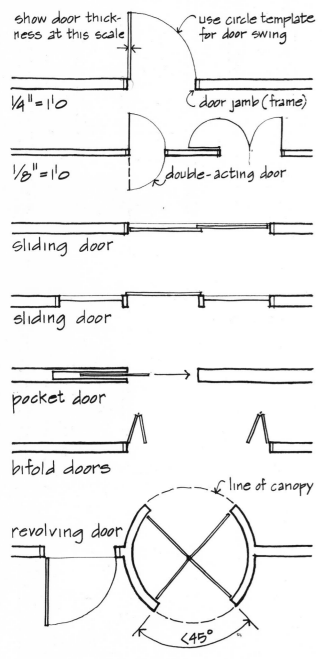

show door thick-
ness at this scale

use circle template
for door swing

1/4" = 1'0

door jamb (frame)

1/8" = 1'0

double-acting door

sliding door

sliding door

pocket door

bifold doors

revolving door

line of canopy

<45°

- show normally swinging doors at a 90° opening, as illustrated
- note that door swings are shown with light lines and quarter circles

- door type (solid wood, wood frame and glass, store front, etc.) is not illustrated in plan, only in elevational views

- window type (double-hung, case-ment, floor to ceiling, etc.) cannot be explained in plan except for width and location - window type and win-dow height are shown in elevational views
- show sill lines with a lighter line weight than walls, jambs, and glass, since sills are not in fact cut through

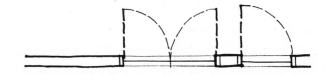

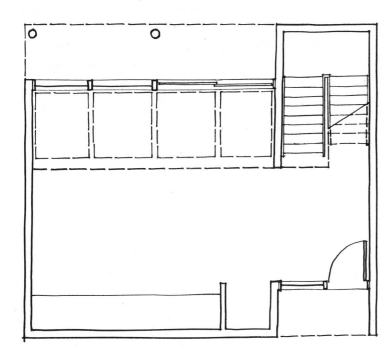

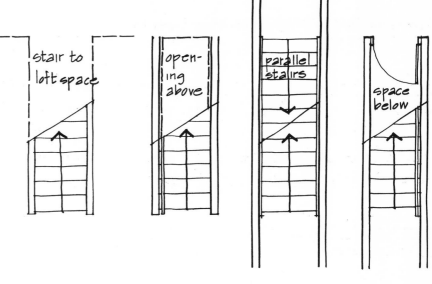

stair to loft space

opening above

parallel stairs

space below

important elements above the horizontal cut (lofts, skylights, roof openings, lowered ceiling areas, roof overhangs, etc.) are indicated by long-dashed lines

----

elements below the floor line are indicated by short-dashed lines

----

to contrast with elements above the plan cut, but they are rarely shown

• show detail such as handrails and toe spaces where scale of drawing permits

• convention to indicate direction of stair: arrow indicates direction (up or down) <u>from</u> level of floor plan

• straight-run stairs

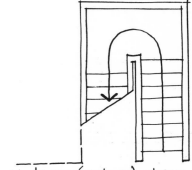

• U-type (return) stair

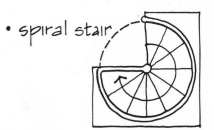

• spiral stair

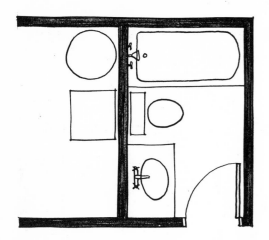

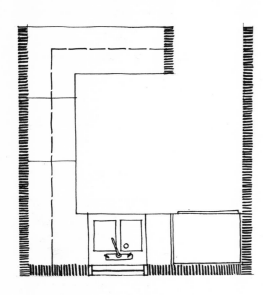

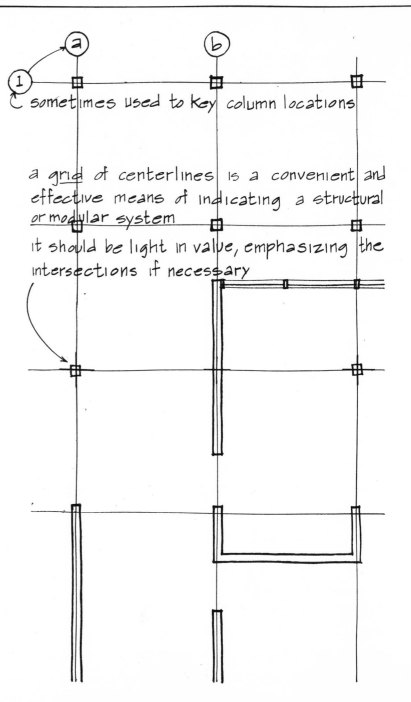

sometimes used to key column locations

a grid of centerlines is a convenient and effective means of indicating a structural or modular system

it should be light in value, emphasizing the intersections if necessary

it should be noted that what is <u>cut through</u> in plan (walls, columns, etc.) takes precedence and should be dominant in value; what is seen <u>within</u> plan (flooring, counters, furniture, etc.) should be lighter in value (see chapter 4 for rendition of values)

The ceiling plan is conventionally a reflected plan of the ceiling so that it has the same orientation as the floor plan. It is drawn as if a large mirror were placed on the floor to reflect the image of the ceiling.

Here, as with the floor plan, a horizontal cut is involved, so all major elements which reach the ceiling should be cut and profiled with a heavy line.

ceiling plan

looking up at ceiling

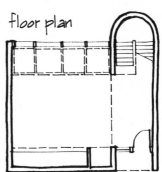
floor plan

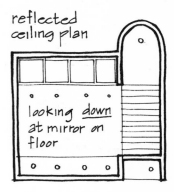
reflected ceiling plan

looking down at mirror on floor

The reflected ceiling plan is used to convey such information as ceiling material and layout, lighting fixtures (type and location), exposed structural members, etc.

The scale of the reflected ceiling plan is usually the same as or smaller than that of the floor plan.

THE ROOF PLAN

The roof plan is simply a view looking straight down at a building, without any cuts involved. It is used to convey the overall roof form and massing within the limits of two-dimensional drawing.

When it is part of a site plan and where time permits, it is recommended that you keep the roof plan simple and give tonal value and texture to the site around the building (see chapter 4).

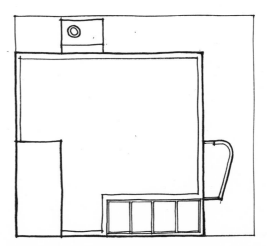

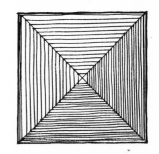

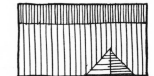

27

The roof plan of a building is usually combined with the <u>site plan</u>, which is intended to illustrate the location and orientation of a building and the environmental context within which it sits.

The site plan is normally drawn at an engineer's scale of 1"= 20', 1"= 30', etc., but may also be shown at 1/16" = 1'0 or 1/8" = 1'0 if detail requires and space permits.

At larger scales, the floor plan may be combined with the site plan if you wish to illustrate the relationship between indoor and outdoor spaces.

SITE ORIENTATION:

The orientation of a building on a site is indicated by a <u>north arrow</u>. Whenever possible, north should be oriented <u>up</u> on a sheet. If a building is oriented less than 45° off the compass points, an assumed north may be used to avoid wordy drawing titles (see page 34).

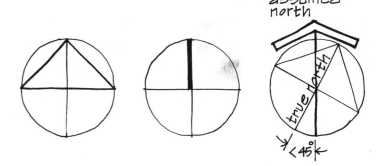

SITE BOUNDARIES:

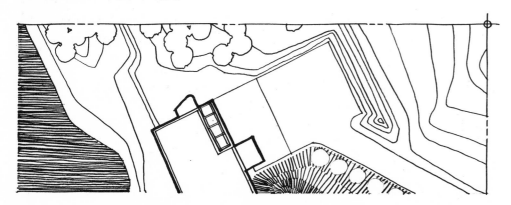

If time permits, a strong contrast in value can be used to indicate site boundaries (see pages 96, 100).

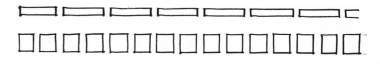

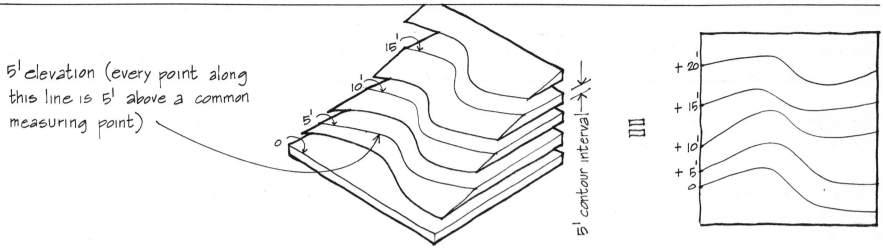

5' elevation (every point along this line is 5' above a common measuring point)

5' contour interval

Contours represent changes in topography in orthographic plan drawings by lines of common elevation. With an understanding of contour lines, the viewer can get a relatively accurate idea of the lay of the land from a two-dimensional site plan.

① equally spaced contours indicate a constant slope
② widely spaced contours indicate relatively flat or very gently sloped land
③ closely spaced contours indicate steeper slopes

The contour interval is determined by the scale of the drawing, the size of the site, and the nature of the topography. The larger the area and the steeper the slopes, the greater the contour interval must be; conversely, for a small site or one with a relatively flat slope, a 5', 2' or even 1' contour may be used.

contour lines are continuous and never cross one another — they coincide only when they indicate a vertical surface

hilltop

depression

retaining wall

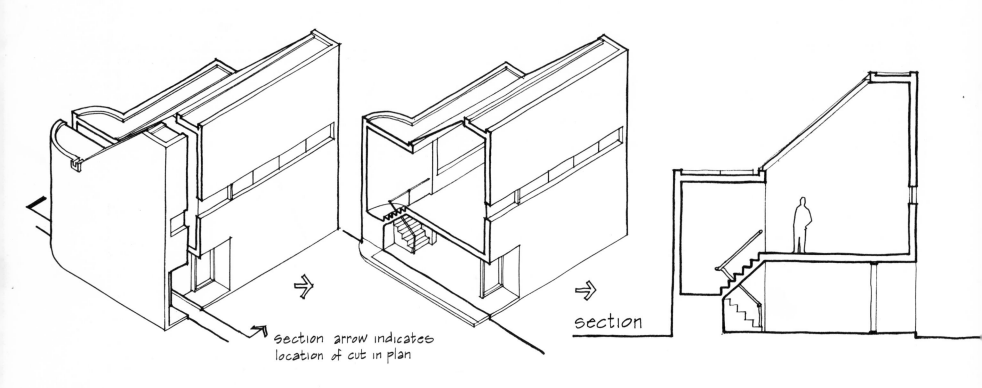

section arrow indicates
location of cut in plan

section

The <u>building section</u> is a <u>horizontal view</u> of a building after a <u>vertical plane</u> has been cut through it
and the front section removed.

<u>Design sections</u>, unlike <u>construction-drawing sections</u>, should always be continuous, using jogs in the
cutting plane only when absolutely necessary. The intent of <u>building design sections</u> is to illustrate
the greatest number of relationships between significant interior spaces; they look toward the most
significant ends of these spaces. One section is usually not sufficient to achieve this unless the
building is extremely simple. (Remember that the building section is only part of a series of related views.)

As with floor plans, whatever is cut through in taking a section (floors, walls, roof structure, etc.) is profiled with a heavy line. What lies behind the cut plane is seen in elevation.

Cut sections through major elements in a building (major window openings, doorways, changes in roof and floor levels, roof openings, fireplaces, etc.). Never cut through columns lest they read as walls!

It is a good practice to include people in building design sections to give scale to the spaces (see pages 90-92).

The physical context of the building should always be shown by indicating the earth upon which it sits, which is also cut through.

Construction details and foundations below grade (ground level) need not be indicated in design sections.

Building sections are normally drawn at 1/8"=1'0 or 1/4"=1'0. For large buildings and complexes, the scale may be reduced to 1/16"=1'0 or smaller. Large scales (3/8"=1'0) are used only for detail design sections.

indicates direction of view
may be broken over a long distance
section indicator in plan

31

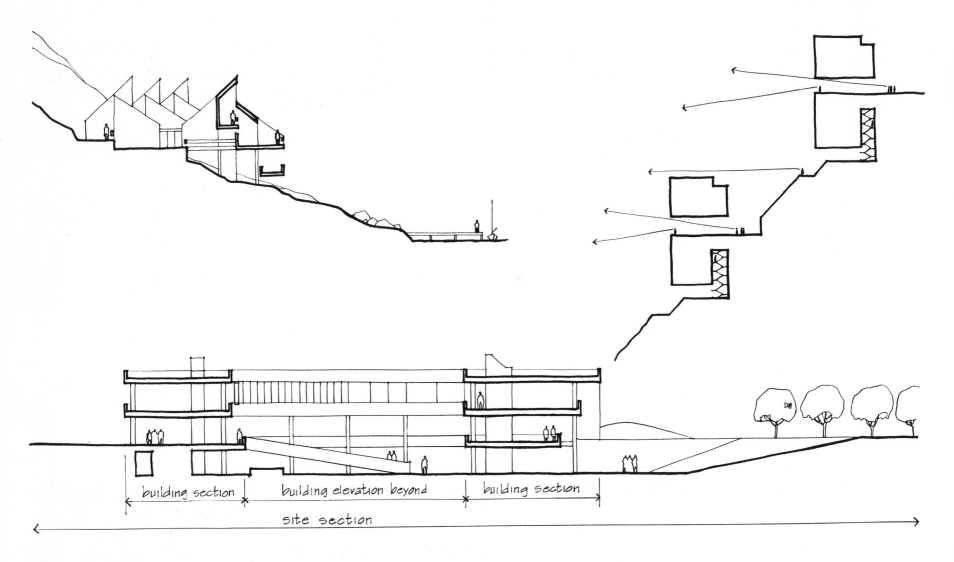

building section   building elevation beyond   building section

site section

Site sections aid in illustrating the environment and physical context of a building, and the relationship between structures and the exterior spaces they define.

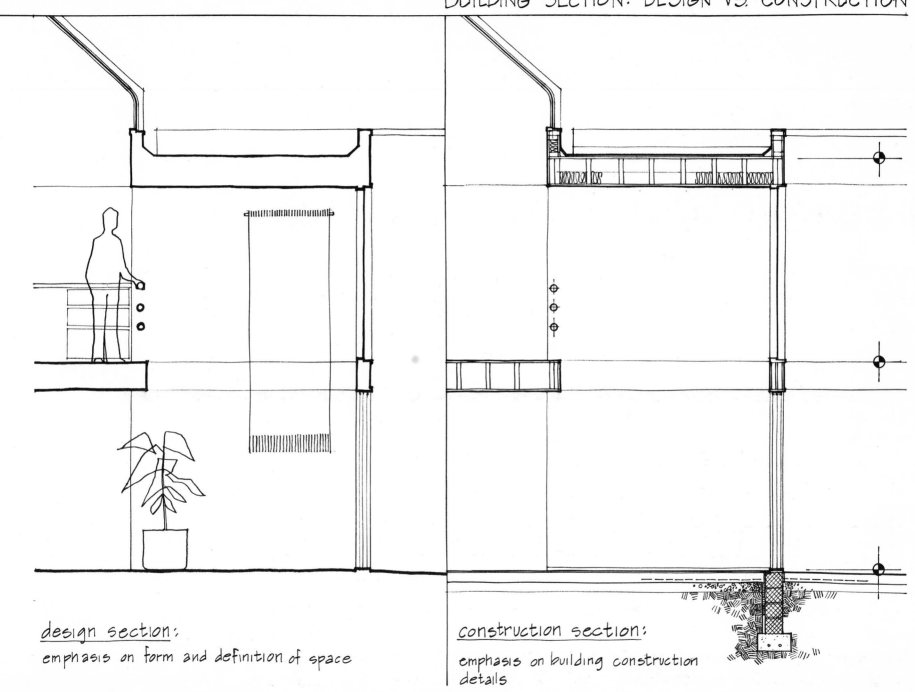

design section:
emphasis on form and definition of space

construction section:
emphasis on building construction details

Architectural elevations of buildings are orthographic drawings of their exteriors from a horizontal point of view. Orthographic projections of a building's interior vertical surfaces, as seen in building sections, are interior elevations.

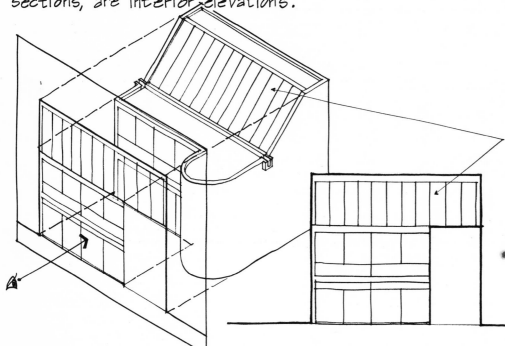

All planar surfaces not parallel to the drawing surface (not perpendicular to the observer's line of sight) appear foreshortened.

All planar surfaces parallel to the drawing surface, and perpendicular to the observer's line of sight retain their true size (to scale), shape, and proportion.

Architectural elevations are labeled in relation to the compass points (see page 28). It is important to note that the face of a building is named for the direction it <u>faces</u> or the direction <u>from which you see it</u>, eg., the north elevation of a building faces north or is the elevation you see from the north. In some instances you may label an elevation with respect to a unique site feature, eg., main street elevation (elevation facing main street) or lake elevation (elevation seen from the lake).

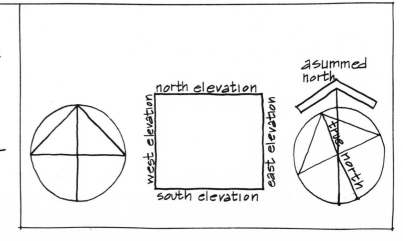

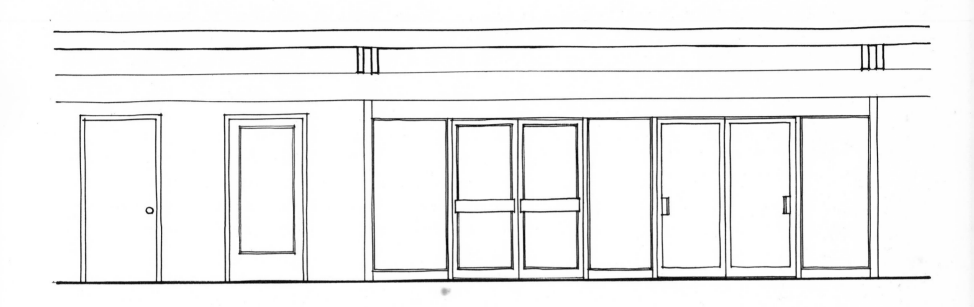

As the scale of a drawing increases, more detail must be shown. Normally, building elevations are drawn at a scale of 1/8"=1'0 or 1/4"=1'0. Large buildings may be shown at 1/16"=1'0 or smaller. For large-scale studies, detail elevations may be shown at 3/8"=1'0 or 3/4"=1'0.

The types of doors and windows illustrated here are not meant to be copied; you must understand the construction of the doors and windows you are drawing and realize that every line you draw represents something in that construction.

Elevation drawings convey a structure's form and massing, door and window openings (type, size, and location), materials, texture, and context. The major difference between building elevations used in construction drawings and those used in design and presentation drawings is in the latter's use of shade and shadows (see pages 84-88) to study what light does to the form and massing of a building.

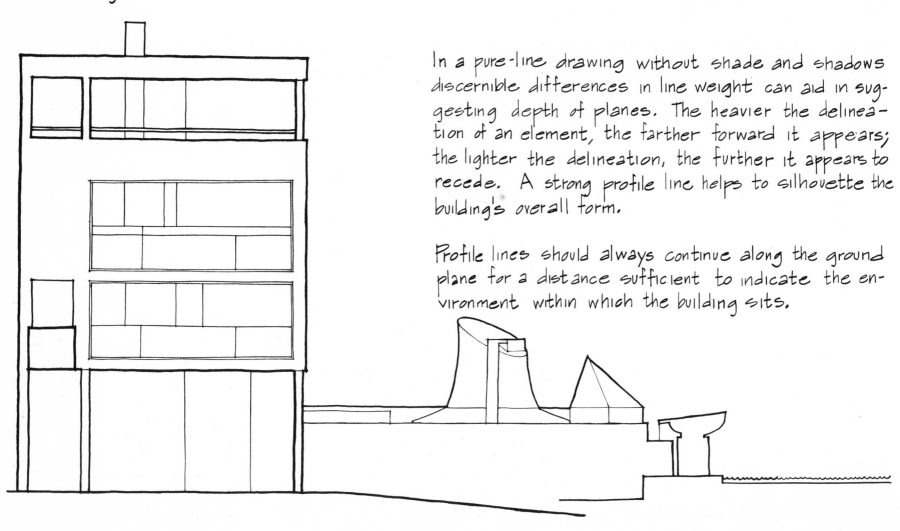

In a pure-line drawing without shade and shadows discernible differences in line weight can aid in suggesting depth of planes. The heavier the delineation of an element, the farther forward it appears; the lighter the delineation, the further it appears to recede. A strong profile line helps to silhouette the building's overall form.

Profile lines should always continue along the ground plane for a distance sufficient to indicate the environment within which the building sits.

While the orthographic drawing conventions, plan/section/elevation, depict reality through a fragmented series of distinct but related views, single-view drawings illustrate the three dimensions of form simultaneously and thus show form relationships in a more realistic manner. For this reason, the two major types of single-view drawings, paraline drawings and perspectives, are called pictorial drawing.

Paraline drawings differ from perspectives in one major way: parallel lines remain parallel in paraline drawings, while they converge to vanishing points in perspectives.

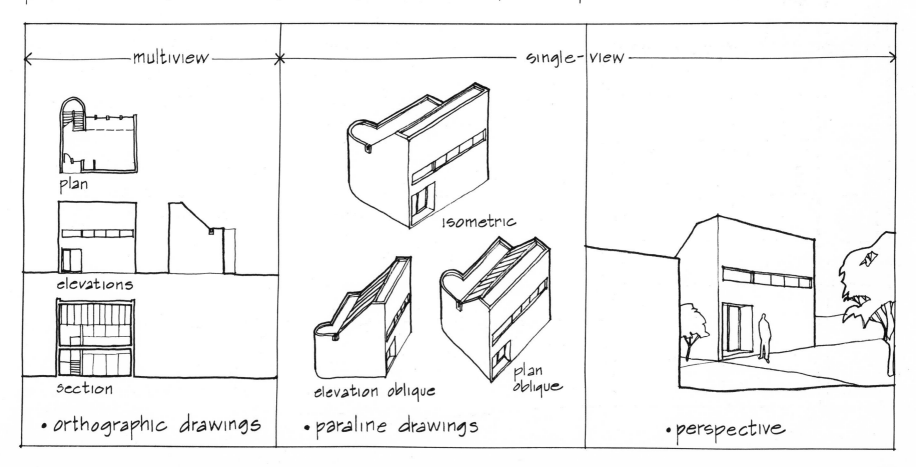

multiview | single-view

plan

elevations

section

• orthographic drawings

isometric

elevation oblique

plan oblique

• paraline drawings

• perspective

TYPES OF PARALINE DRAWINGS

There are a number of paraline drawings, which are named after the method of projection that is used to develop them. Two of the most common in architectural drawing are discussed in this section: isometric and oblique (in terms of both plan and elevation).

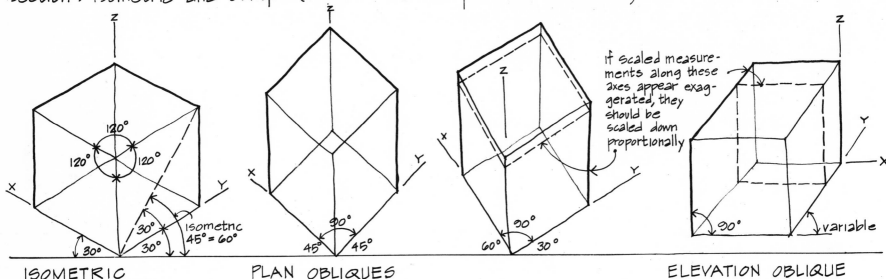

ISOMETRIC

- all three visible surfaces have equal emphasis

- relatively inflexible

- orthographic plans and elevations can never be used in an isometric drawing

PLAN OBLIQUES

- a 45°-45° oblique has a higher angle of view than an isometric, and horizontal planes receive more emphasis

- a 30°-60° oblique also has a high angle of view with one vertical plane receiving more emphasis than the other

- in plan obliques, orthographic plan views can be utilized - this is advantageous in showing the true form of horizontal planes and in depicting circular forms in plan

ELEVATION OBLIQUE

- a vertical plane remains parallel to the drawing surface, showing itself in true size (to scale), shape, and proportion - this face of the building should be the length of the building, the most significant face, or the most complex

In the above drawings:
① all vertical lines remain vertical
② all parallel lines remain parallel
③ all lines parallel to x·y·z axes can be drawn to scale

Circles in nonfrontal planes in paraline drawings appear as ellipses. With the four-center method (using two sets of radii and a compass or circle template) you can approximate an ellipse that is usually close enough to a true ellipse to suit most purposes.

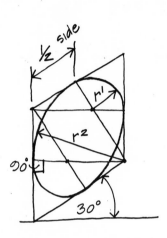
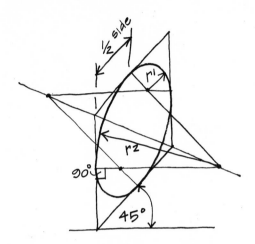
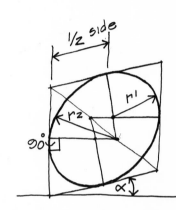

CONSTRUCTION: ① draw circumscribing square axonometrically

② at the midpoints of the sides of the axonometric square draw perpendiculars and extend them until they intersect

③ with these points of intersection as centers and with radii r^1 and r^2 equal to the respective lengths of the perpendiculars, describe two sets of arcs in equal pairs between the points where the perpendiculars originate

For freeform curvilinear lines you can use a grid along the appropriate pair of axes to plot the points of intersection in the paraline drawing.

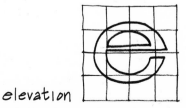

elevation   isometric

For most rectilinear forms the construction of a paraline drawing is relatively simple, since all lines parallel to the X·Y·Z axes (axonometric lines) are to scale and all parallel lines remain parallel. Standard 30°·30°, 45°·45°, and 30°·60° orientations for the X·Y base axes also aid in the construction of a paraline drawing.

Nonaxonometric lines (lines not parallel to the X·Y·Z axes) are <u>not</u> to scale; the axonometric ends of non-axonometric lines must first be located, and then the nonaxonometric lines are drawn between these points:

① enclose the irregular form in a rectilinear box
② using the edges of this box as measuring lines, locate the ends of the nonaxonometric lines through the use of offset measurements

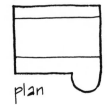

plan

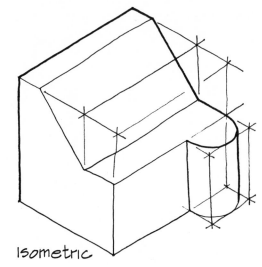

Isometric

The major pictorial defect of an axonometric drawing is that parallel lines appear to diverge as they recede in apparent contradiction to what we normally see in perspective. For this reason excessive lengths in the X or Y dimensions should be avoided.

Cubic forms and 45° lines sometimes appear flat in isometric drawings (an optical illusion). In such cases a plan oblique may be preferable.

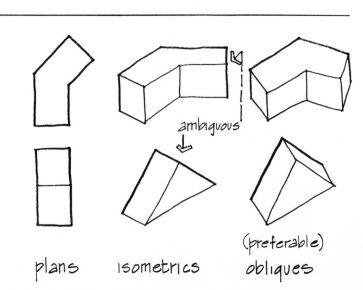

ambiguous

(preferable)

plans   isometrics   obliques

Paraline drawings are particularly useful in architectural graphics because of their ease of construction (both drafted and freehand) and their effectiveness as a pictorial view. Most people find paraline drawings easy to understand, since they resemble natural perception more closely than orthographic drawings.

The following are examples of some of the ways paraline drawings are used:

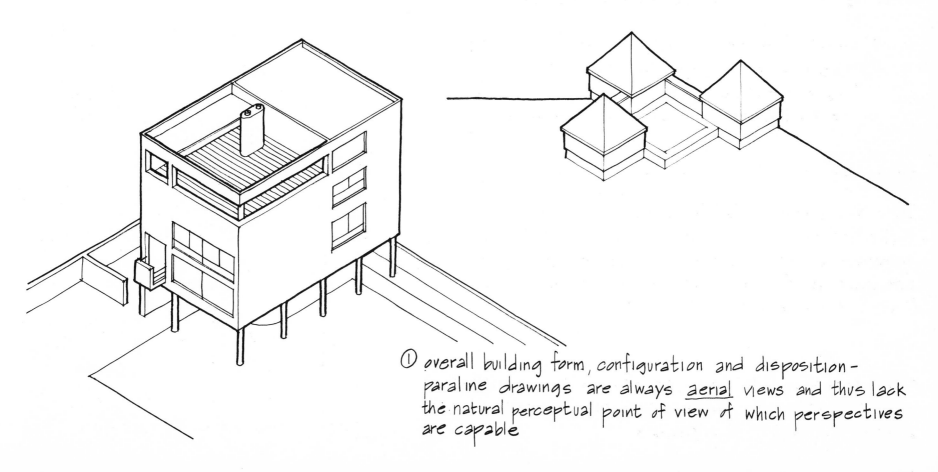

① overall building form, configuration and disposition - paraline drawings are always <u>aerial</u> views and thus lack the natural perceptual point of view of which perspectives are capable

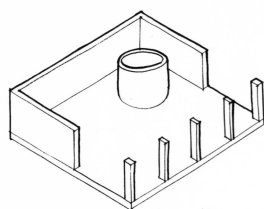

• an isometric such as this can be deceptive, since the walls tend to be read at full height - always draw walls at full height

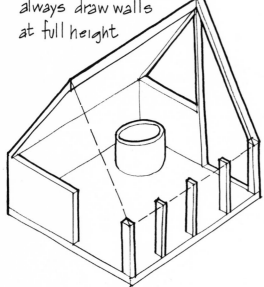

• always indicate the overall form of the building and space within - the less you cut away from the total form, the more comprehensible the true nature of the form is

• for circles in plan, it is easier to use a plan oblique than an isometric, since the orthographic plan is used as the base drawing and horizontal circles remain true circles

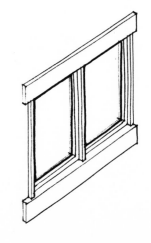

② building cutaways
to illustrate interiors

③ illustrating building details
as with other scale drawings, the larger the scale, the more detail you have to show

HIERARCHY OF LINES:

① profile of total field of each floor level—
   do not profile ground line
② horizontal-cut lines
③ profile lines of individual elements—
   edges against space (see page 75)
④ transitions in form (corners)
⑤ material texture
⑥ vertical (light or dashed) lines to
   reinforce vertical relationships of
   structure/circulation/form

giving the horizontal floor planes a
tonal value or texture aids in the
definition of vertical elements

any overlap between floor levels
should not cover significant
information

④ <u>Expanded views</u> are especially useful in
illustrating vertical relationships in multistory
buildings

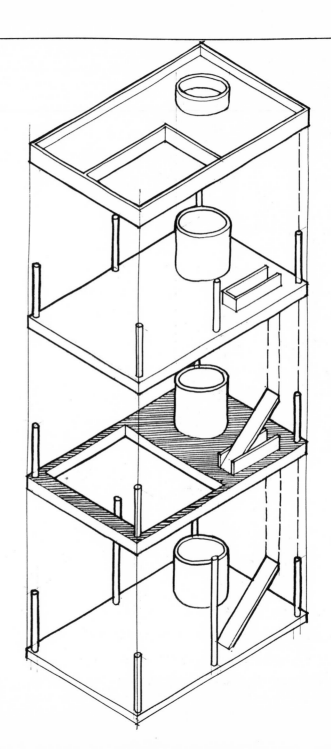

Perspective is the third major type of drawing in architectural graphics. Like a paraline drawing, the perspective is a single-view drawing. Unlike the former, however, a correctly drawn perspective eliminates the optical distortion of lines drawn in parallel and is generally more readily understood, since it, more than any other drawing type, represents the reality of form in three dimensions as we naturally perceive it.

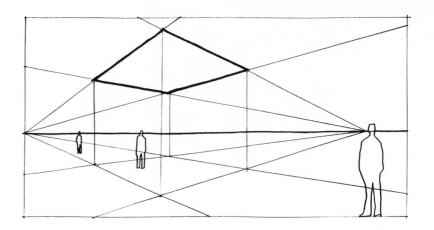

In drawing a perspective, we project on a flat surface the correct oblique aspects of a form as they appear to an observer. In other words, a correctly drawn perspective is the two-dimensional representation of the appearance (ie. what we see) of an object, as opposed to the reality (ie. what we know) of that object. The better we understand the form of an object, the easier it is for us to draw it in proper perspective.

Perspective drawings possess four major characteristics, which are utilized to portray a sense of space, depth, and the third dimension within the limits of a two-dimensional drawing:

    ① overlapping of forms
    ② diminution of size
    ③ convergence of parallel lines
    ④ foreshortening

(the latter three characteristics distinguish perspective drawings from both orthographic and paraline drawings)

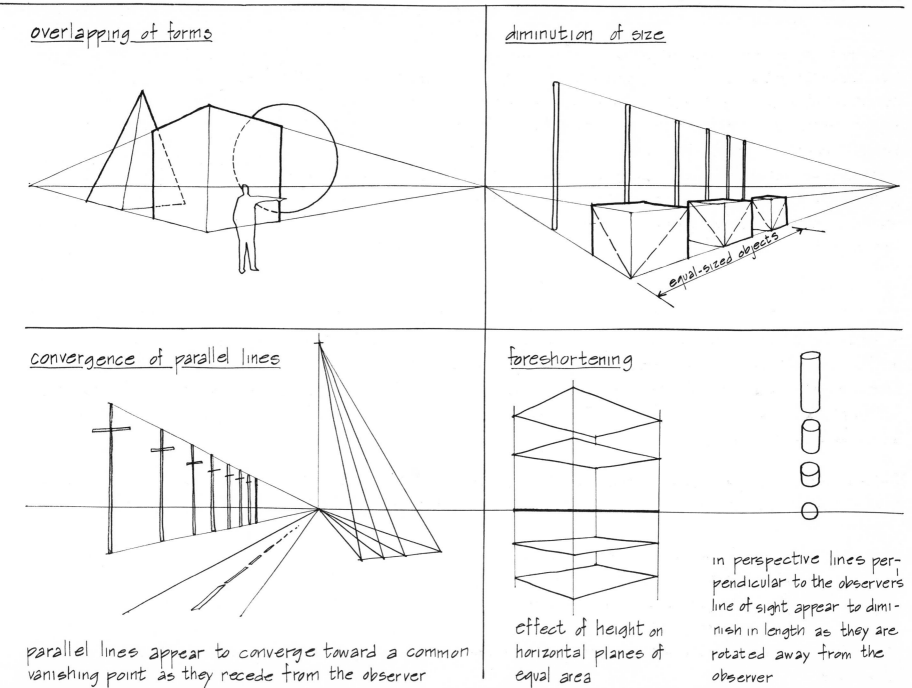

overlapping of forms

diminution of size

equal-sized objects

convergence of parallel lines

foreshortening

effect of height on horizontal planes of equal area

parallel lines appear to converge toward a common vanishing point as they recede from the observer

in perspective lines perpendicular to the observers line of sight appear to diminish in length as they are rotated away from the observer

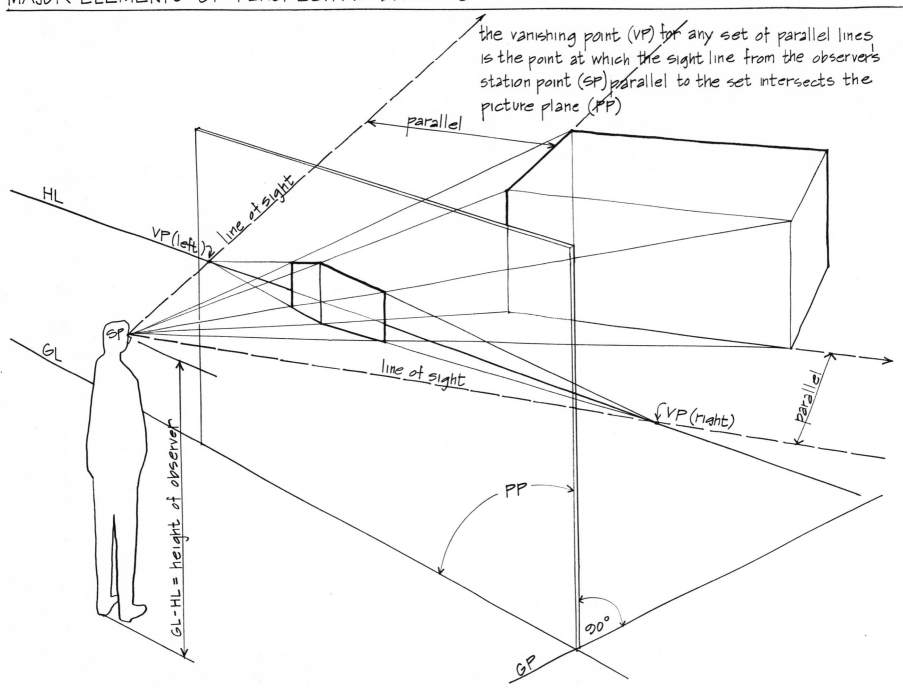

the vanishing point (VP) for any set of parallel lines is the point at which the sight line from the observer's station point (SP) parallel to the set intersects the picture plane (PP)

parallel

line of sight

HL

VP (left)

SP

GL

GL-HL = height of observer

line of sight

VP (right)

parallel

PP

GP

20°

station point (SP): the position and orientation of the observer; the pictorial effect obtained in a perspective drawing is determined by the position of SP, its distance from what is viewed, and the angle of view

center of view (c): the orthographic projection of SP (eye of the observer) onto the picture plane

cone of vision: the maximum angle of vision (45°-60°) within which what is viewed is in focus; everything of importance to be drawn in perspective should be within this cone of vision, since it would otherwise be subject to excessive distortion

circles and spherical forms in perspective should fall within a 30° cone of vision if possible

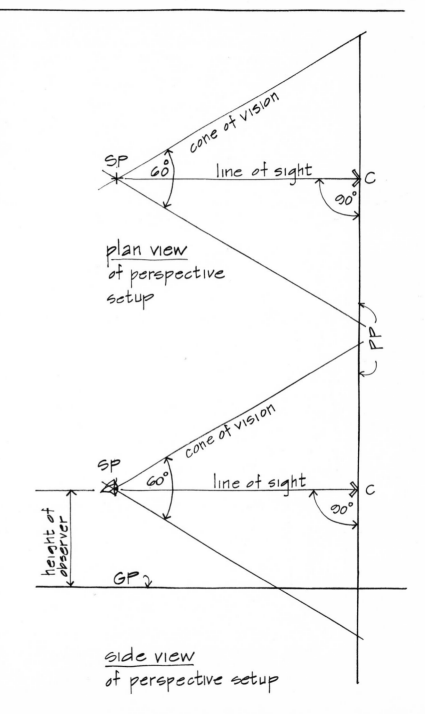

plan view
of perspective
setup

side view
of perspective setup

horizon line (HL): a horizontal line lying within the picture plane (perpendicular to the observer's line of sight) at the same height as the eye of the observer (SP); the center of vision (C), therefore, is always coincidental with the horizon line

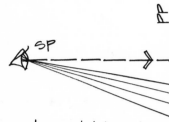

PP

C is always coincidental with HL (seen here in end view)

all horizontal lines appear to vanish on the horizon line

as the base horizontal line is extended to infinity, the intersection of the observer's sight rays and the picture plane will approach the horizon line

SP

horizontal base line

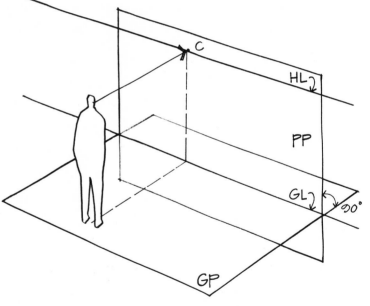

ground plane (GP): the horizontal reference plane from which vertical measurements are taken; the height of the horizon line (HL) above the ground plane is always equal to the height of the observer (SP) above the ground plane

ground line (GL): the intersection of the ground plane and the picture plane; the ground line is used primarily as a measuring line (ML)

picture plane (PP): the transparent, two-dimensional plane, perpendicular to the observer's line of sight, through which the observer views what is seen in perspective (see page 46); the perspective of any point is always at the point on the picture plane where the observer's line of sight to the point in question pierces the picture plane; in practice, the picture plane is coincidental with the drawing surface upon which the perspective drawing is executed

vanishing points (VP): all sets of parallel lines (not parallel to the picture plane) appear in perspective to converge toward a <u>common vanishing point</u>

each set of parallel lines has its own vanishing point:

① all sets of parallel <u>horizontal</u> lines appear to converge on the horizon line

② a set of parallel lines sloping downward and away from the observer has its vanishing point <u>below</u> the horizon line; conversely, a set of parallel lines rising upward and away from the observer has its vanishing point <u>above</u> the horizon line

③ all lines parallel to the picture plane do <u>not</u> converge but rather retain their true orientation

SIZE/SHAPE/DIRECTION OF LINES AND PLANES IN PERSPECTIVE:

① all lines lying within the picture plane retain their true length (to scale) and direction
all planes lying within the picture plane retain their true size (to scale), shape, and orientation

② all lines parallel to the picture plane retain their true direction but increase in apparent length as they come in front of it and decrease in apparent length as they recede from it
all planes parallel to the picture plane retain their true shape and orientation, but their apparent size likewise increases as they move in front of it and decreases as they recede from it

③ all lines and planes not parallel to the picture plane are <u>never</u> shown in true size (to scale), shape, or direction

The observer's _point of view_ (angle of view, height, and distance from object and picture plane) is critical in determining the final pictorial effect of the perspective drawing. The following four pages illustrate how the positions of the station point (the observer), the picture plane, and the object with respect to one another affect the final perspective drawing.

① height of station point with respect to object

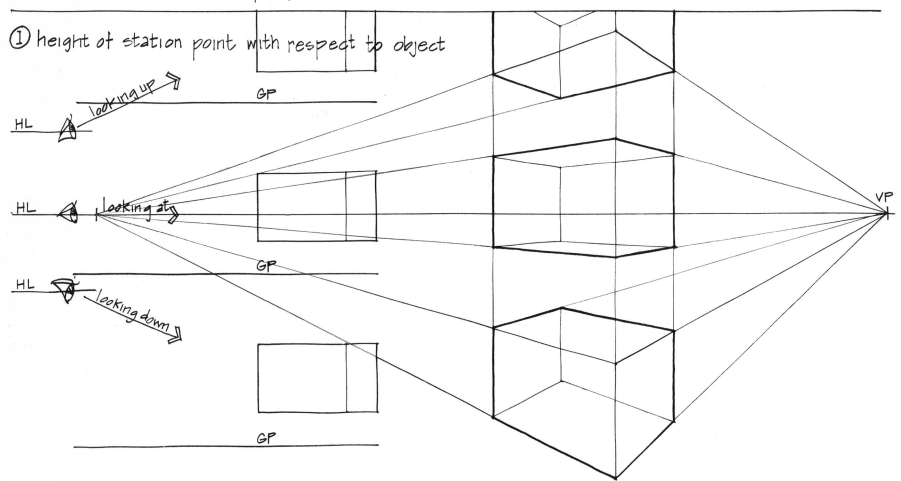

The height of the observer (and therefore the horizon line) with respect to the object viewed determines whether the object is seen from above, below, or within its own height. As the eye of the observer moves up or down, the horizon line and the vanishing points on it move up or down with it.

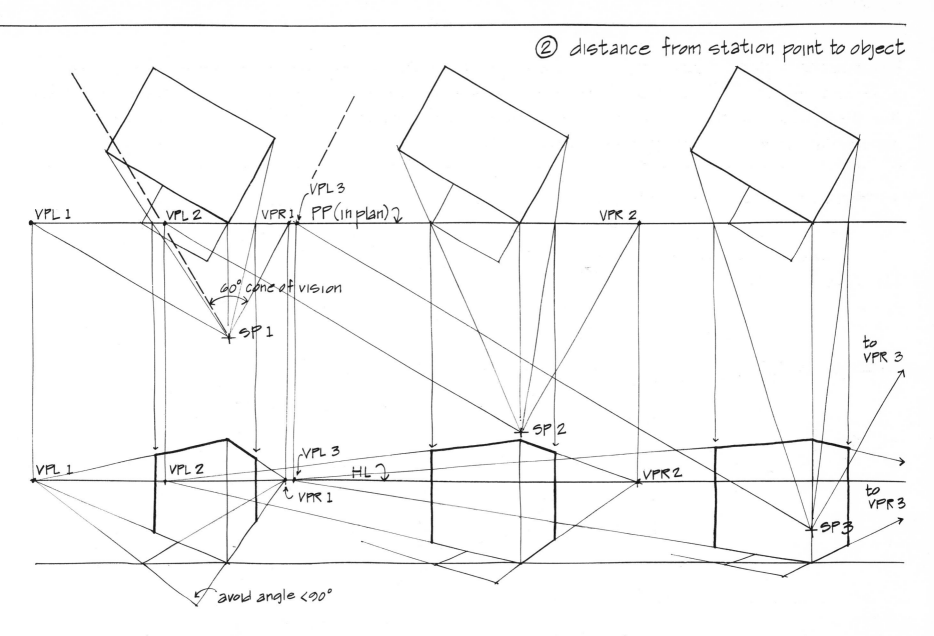

VPL 1 VPL 2 VPR 1 VPL 3 PP (in plan)

VPR 2

60° cone of vision

SP 1

to VPR 3

SP 2

VPL 1 VPL 2 VPL 3 HL VPR 2

VPR 1

to VPR 3

SP 3

avoid angle <90°

The distance from the station point to the object influences the rate of foreshortening in the final perspective. As the distance from the object increases, the vanishing points move farther apart, the horizontal lines flatten out, and the perspective depth is compressed.

③ position of the picture plane

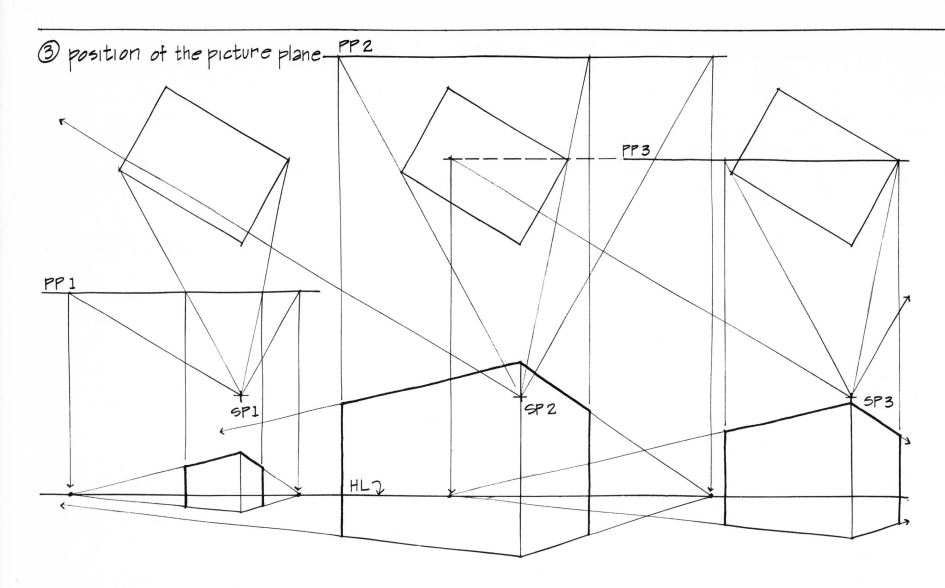

The size of the final perspective image obtained with a given object, a given scale, and a given relationship between station point and object can be varied by changing the position of the picture plane. The nearer the picture plane is to the station point, the smaller the image; the farther the picture plane is from the station point, the larger the image. If all positions of the picture plane are parallel, the resulting perspective images are identical in all respects except size.

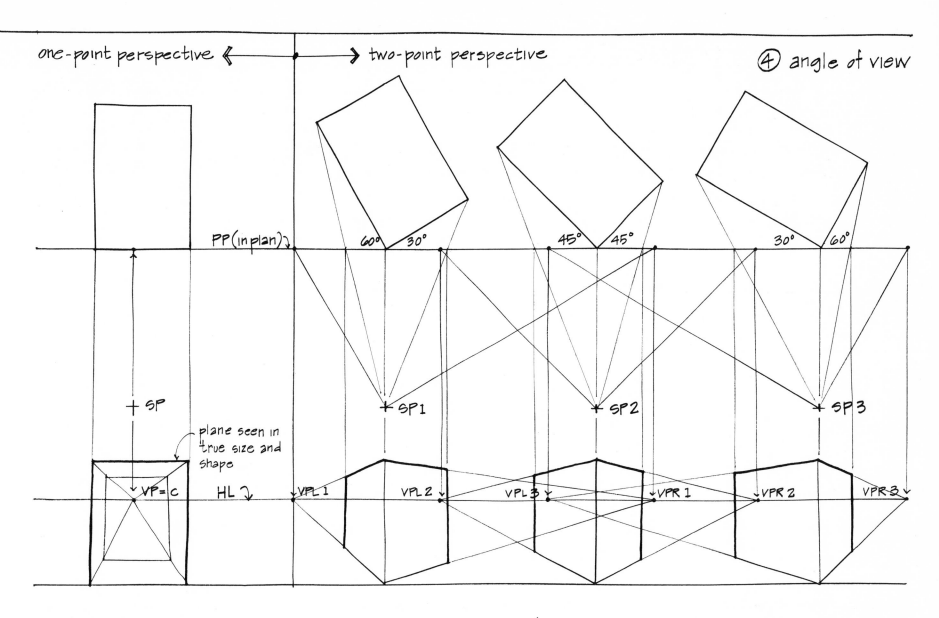

one-point perspective ⟨   ⟶ two-point perspective

④ angle of view

PP (in plan)

60° 30°   45° 45°   30° 60°

+ SP   ☆ SP1   ☆ SP2   ☆ SP3

plane seen in true size and shape

↘ VP = C   HL ↴   ↓VPL 1   ↓VPL 2   ↓VPL 3   ↓VPR 1   ↓VPR 2   ↓VPR 3 ↘

The orientation of the object with respect to the observer's line of sight and the picture plane affects the degree of foreshortening of the various facets of that object. The more frontal a plane is to the picture plane, the less it is foreshortened. Ultimately, when a plane becomes parallel to the picture plane, it is seen in its true shape and orientation.

TYPES OF PERSPECTIVE

Depending <u>solely</u> on the observer's <u>point of view</u> and the orientation of the object viewed, there are three basic types of perspective drawings:

① one-point perspective occurs when one major set of parallel lines lies <u>parallel</u> to the picture plane (perpendicular to the observer's line of sight); the vertical (z axis) and horizontal (x axis) lines within these planes remain vertical and horizontal, while the other major set of horizontal lines (Y axis), being <u>perpendicular</u> to the picture plane, vanishes on the horizon line at one point (c)

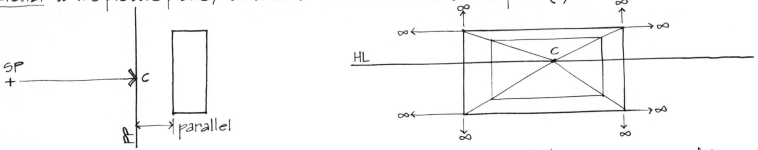

② two-point perspective retains the verticality of vertical lines, but both major sets of horizontal lines (x·y axes) are <u>oblique</u> to the picture plane, and both sets have their own vanishing points

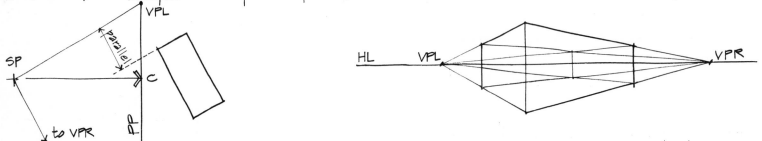

③ three-point perspective has all three major sets of lines (x·y·z axes) oblique to the picture plane and therefore has three major vanishing points

---

Regardless of the specific type of perspective, the characteristics, elements, and principles mentioned heretofore remain applicable and relevant. It should be noted that any perspective may have any number of vanishing points. The terminology used in categorizing types of perspectives refers only to <u>major</u> vanishing points.

One-point perspectives are useful in portraying interior spaces, some street scenes, and axial arrangements. They are relatively easy to construct but can result in dull and static views.

The following is a method of constructing a space grid in perspective which enables you to lay out a one-point perspective of an interior space.

Before beginning the construction of any perspective, you must first determine your desired point of view: what do you wish to illustrate and why?

① after you determine the space you are going to illustrate, the station point and the observer's point of view must be fixed in plan

PP

the position of PP relative to SP determines the final size of the perspective image (see page 52); the most advantageous position of PP for ease of construction is coincidental with a major plane perpendicular to the observer's line of sight

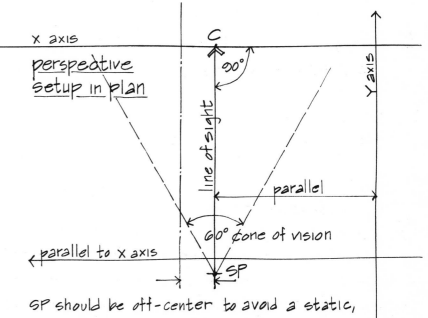

perspective setup in plan

since this is a one-point perspective, the observer's line of sight should be parallel to one major axis of the space and perpendicular to the other

SP should be far enough back of the space so that the majority of it lies within the cone of vision

SP should be off-center to avoid a static, symmetrical perspective image

② since anything within the picture plane can be scaled (see page 49), draw the overall configuration of the wall plane coincidental with the picture plane at any appropriate scale (the scale of this picture-plane wall does not need to be at the same scale as the plan setup in ①; it should be selected according to the desired size of the perspective image and the amount of detail you wish to show

③ at the same scale of the picture-plane wall, draw a horizontal line to represent the horizon line, which is always assumed to be at the same level as the eye of the observer; for interiors, this may be 4'-5', depending on whether emphasis is to be placed on the floor plane or ceiling (see page 50).

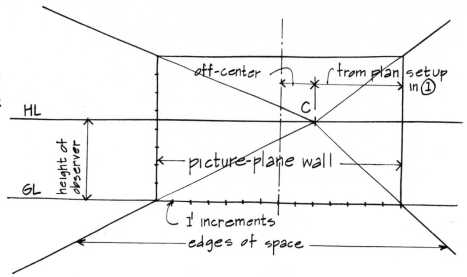

④ locate the observer's center of vision; its horizontal position along the horizon line relative to the sides of the space can be determined from the plan setup in ①

⑤ draw lines from the center of vision through the major corners of the picture-plane wall to establish the major edges of the space and begin to define it

⑥ tick off 1' increments along the sides and bottom of the picture-plane wall (this is possible since anything within the picture plane can be scaled)

1' increments are used here as an example; the increments may be increased if it is not necessary to have a very detailed drawing

⑦ through these marks draw lines from the center of vision

⑧ from the center of vision measure to scale a distance (left or right) along the horizon line equivalent to the distance from the station point to the center of vision in plan (see ①); call this point on the horizon line a diagonal point (DP) (left or right); both left and right diagonal points serve the same purpose

the diagonal point is a vanishing point for 45° lines which cut off equal sides of right triangles, enabling you to scale depth measurements in perspective

⑨ from the diagonal point draw a line through the two bottom corners of the picture - plane wall

⑩ where these two lines cut across the 1' lines on the floor plane, vanishing at the center of vision, draw <u>horizontal</u> lines

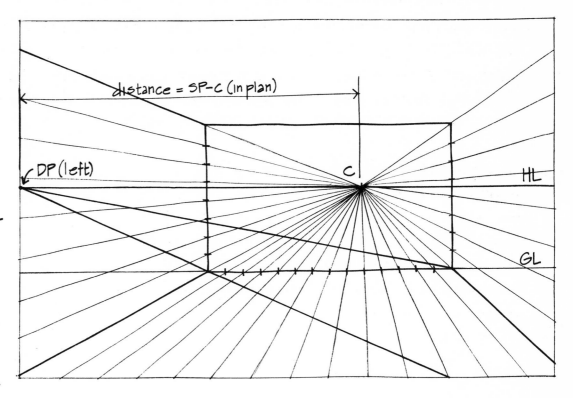

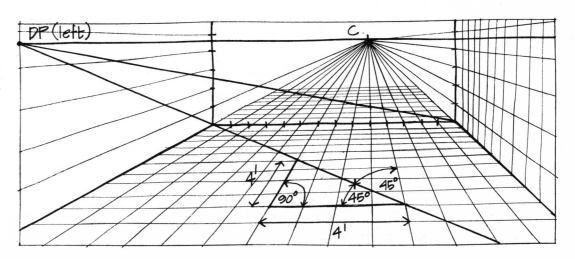

⑪ you have now established a grid of 1' squares on the floor plane ; if you feel there is too much distortion (ie, if the squares become too exaggerated in depth) in the foreground or along the foreground corners, move the diagonal point further out along the horizon line from the center of vision and repeat ⑨ and ⑩ (note that if you move the diagonal point further away from the center of vision, you are in effect moving the observer away from the space and increasing the area of the space within the observer's cone of vision)

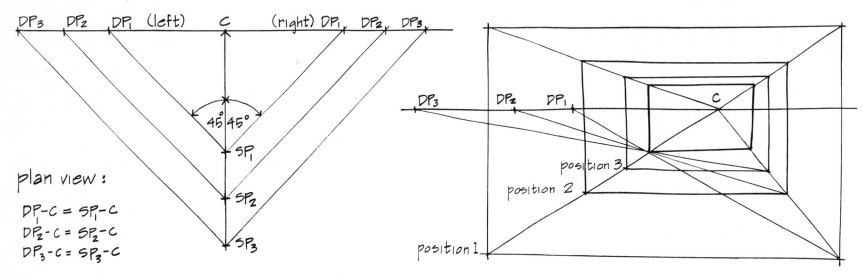

plan view :

$DP_1 - C = SP_1 - C$
$DP_2 - C = SP_2 - C$
$DP_3 - C = SP_3 - C$

⑫ from where the horizontal lines of the floor grid meet the side walls of the space, draw verticals

you have now established a grid of 1' squares along the two side-wall planes and the floor plane of the space being drawn

With this perspective grid as a base you can lay a piece of tracing paper over it and draw in the major architectural elements of the space. With the same grid you can also locate the positions and relative sizes of other elements within the space, such as light fixtures and furniture.

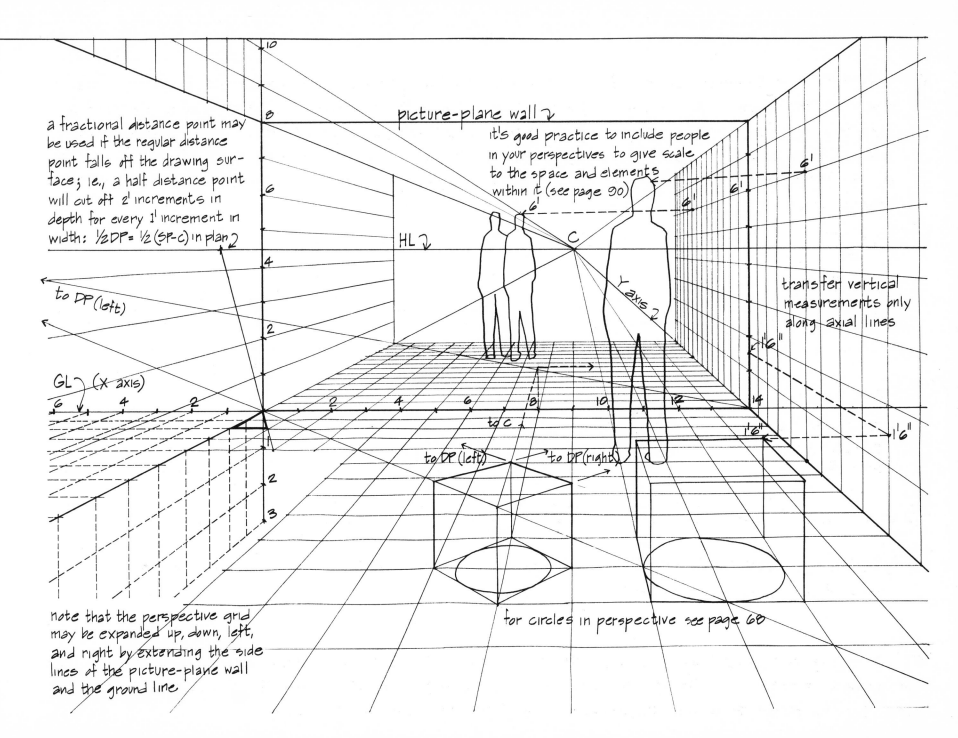

a fractional distance point may
be used if the regular distance
point falls off the drawing surface; ie., a half distance point
will cut off 2' increments in
depth for every 1' increment in
width: ½ DP= ½ (SP-c) in plan

picture-plane wall

it's good practice to include people
in your perspectives to give scale
to the space and elements
within it (see page 90)

6'   6'
6'   6'   6'

HL

C

Y axis

to DP (left)

transfer vertical
measurements only
along axial lines

1'6"

GL   (X axis)

6   4   2   2   4   6   8   10   12   14

1'6"

to c

to DP (left)   to DP(right)

1'6"

2

3

note that the perspective grid
may be expanded up, down, left,
and right by extending the side
lines of the picture-plane wall
and the ground line

for circles in perspective see page 60

TWO-POINT PERSPECTIVE

Two-point perspective is probably the most widely used of the three perspective-drawing types. Unlike one-point perspective a two-point perspective tends to be neither symmetrical nor static, and it portrays a more natural view for the observer. It is used for both interior and exterior spaces and forms, and is readily adaptable to most situations.

The following is a method of constructing a space grid in two-point perspective, utilizing measuring points (MP).

As with the construction of a one-point perspective, you must first establish the observer's point of view. Determine what you wish to illustrate. Look toward the most significant areas and try to visualize from your plan drawing what will be seen in the foreground, middle-ground, and background. Review the previous discussion on the effects of the height of the station point, the distance from the station point to the object, the position of the picture plane, and the observer's angle of view on the final perspective drawing (pages 50-53).

① at a convenient scale in plan:

- lay out the major outline of the space or form

- locate the station point, being careful that most of what you wish to illustrate lies within the 60° cone of vision

- locate the picture plane (always perpendicular to the observer's line of sight)
  it is usually convenient to run it through a major vertical element (a corner or a column) so that it can be used as a vertical measuring line

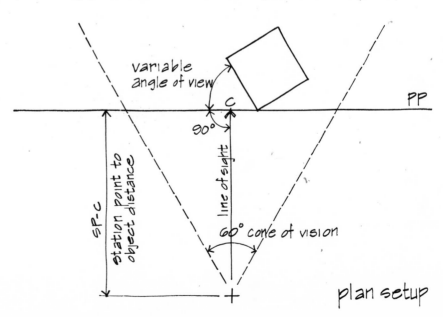

plan setup

② determine:

- vanishing point left   (VPL)
- vanishing point right (VPR)
- measuring point left   (MPL)
- measuring point right (MPR)
- center of vision   (C)

- vanishing point for any line is the point at which a line from the station point parallel to the line in question intersects the picture plane

- in this plan setup include vanishing points for secondary lines which might be useful in constructing your perspective (ie., if you have a series of 45° lines in your design, find their vanishing point [VP (45°)] as shown

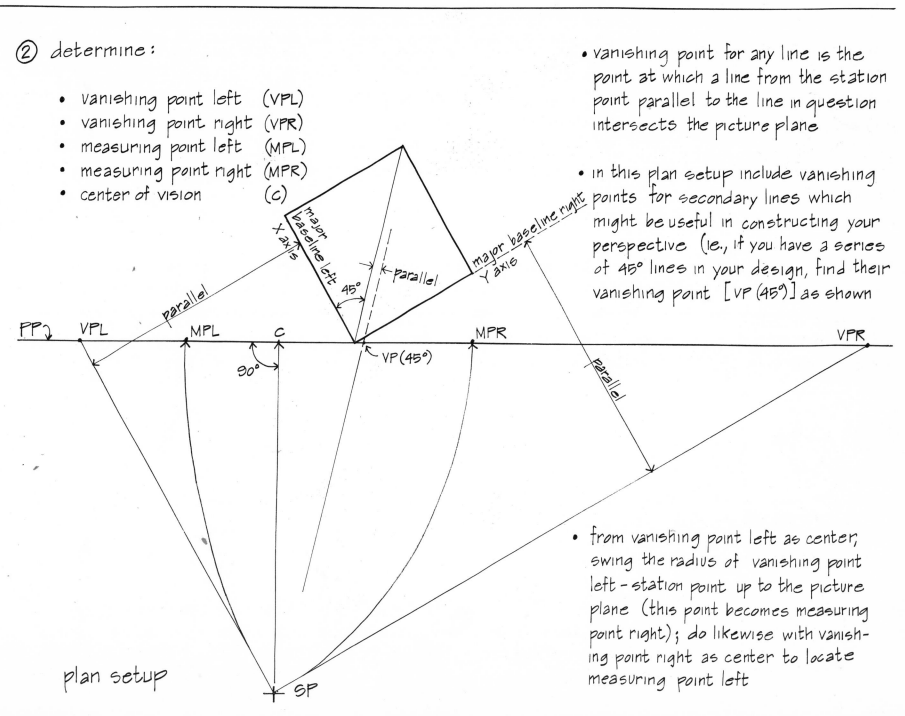

- from vanishing point left as center, swing the radius of vanishing point left – station point up to the picture plane (this point becomes measuring point right); do likewise with vanishing point right as center to locate measuring point left

plan setup

③ in perspective and at an appropriate scale (which need not be the same scale as the perspective setup in plan) lay out the horizon line and determine on this line the points previously laid out in plan and wherever the form or space might touch or intersect the picture plane

④ where the picture plane cuts across the form or space as determined in the perspective setup in plan, draw a vertical line; this line, since it lies within the picture plane, can be scaled and is therefore called a vertical measuring line (VML)

where this vertical meets the ground plane is determined by the height of the eye of the observer; from this point, a horizontal ground line (GL) can be drawn (this line also lies within the picture plane and can also be scaled)

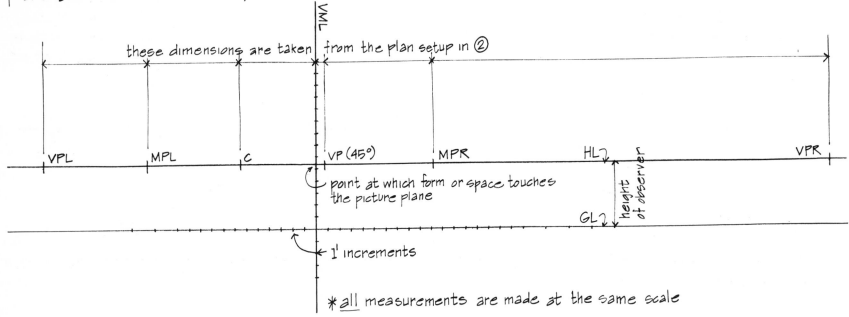

these dimensions are taken from the plan setup in ②

VML

VPL   MPL   C   VP (45°)   MPR   HL⌐   height of observer   VPR

⌐ point at which form or space touches the picture plane

GL⌐

↑ 1' increments

* all measurements are made at the same scale

⑤ scale off 1' measurements along the ground line and the vertical measuring line

⑥ from the left and right vanishing points draw lines through the intersection of the ground line and the vertical measuring line
these are the <u>major baselines</u> (X·Y axes) in perspective

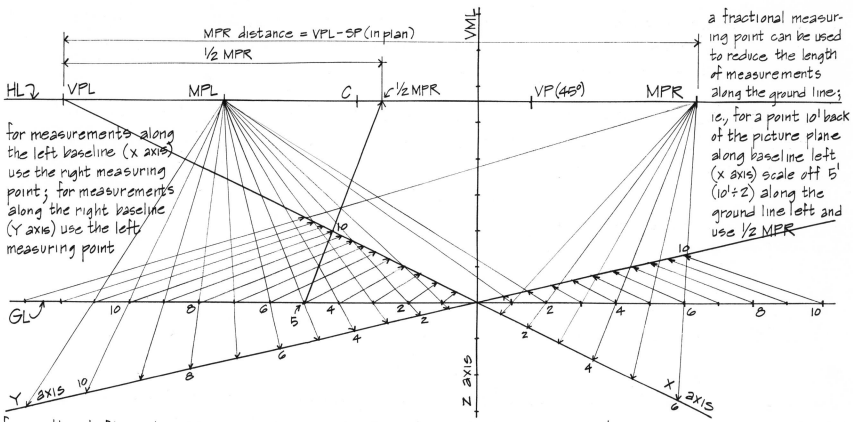

MPR distance = VPL−SP (in plan)

½ MPR

a fractional measuring point can be used to reduce the length of measurements along the ground line;

ie., for a point 10' back of the picture plane along baseline left (x axis) scale off 5' (10'÷2) along the ground line left and use ½ MPR

HL

VPL   MPL   C   ½ MPR   VP(45°)   MPR   VML

for measurements along the left baseline (x axis) use the right measuring point; for measurements along the right baseline (Y axis) use the left measuring point

GL

Y axis   10   8   6   5   4   2   2   2   2   4   6   8   10   X axis
                                                    4   2
                                        6   4
                              8   6
                        10   10

Z axis

⑦ from the left and right <u>measuring points</u> draw lines to the scaled 1' increments along the ground line

these are <u>construction</u> lines that are used only to <u>transfer</u> scaled measurements along the ground line to the major baselines in perspective (as you can see, equal measurements in perspective appear to diminish in size as they recede from the observer)

⑧ from the left and right vanishing points draw grid lines through the transferred measurements along the major baselines in perspective and the scaled measurements along the vertical measuring line

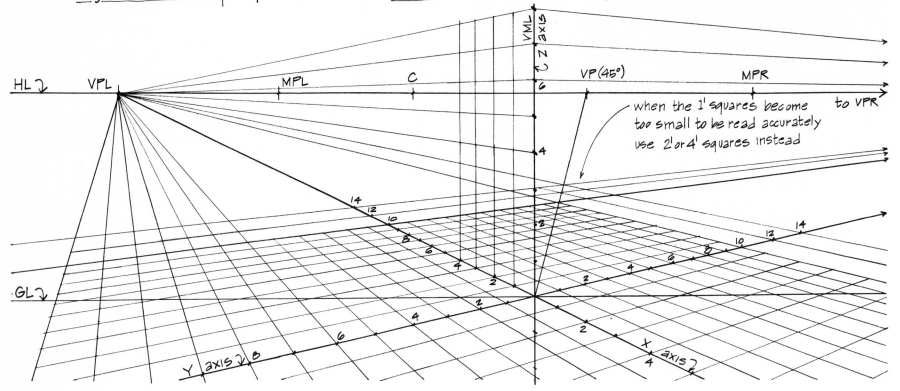

when the 1' squares become too small to be read accurately use 2' or 4' squares instead

This perspective grid which you have just constructed is correct for your selected point of view and its specific station point/picture plane/object relationships (see pages 50-53). If an aerial view is desired, for example, then the grid would be constructed with identical relationships of those elements along the horizon line, but the ground line would be lowered to make the distance between the two equal to the height of the observer above the ground.

It is good practice to save the perspective grids you construct for possible future use. File them under height of observer and angle of view.

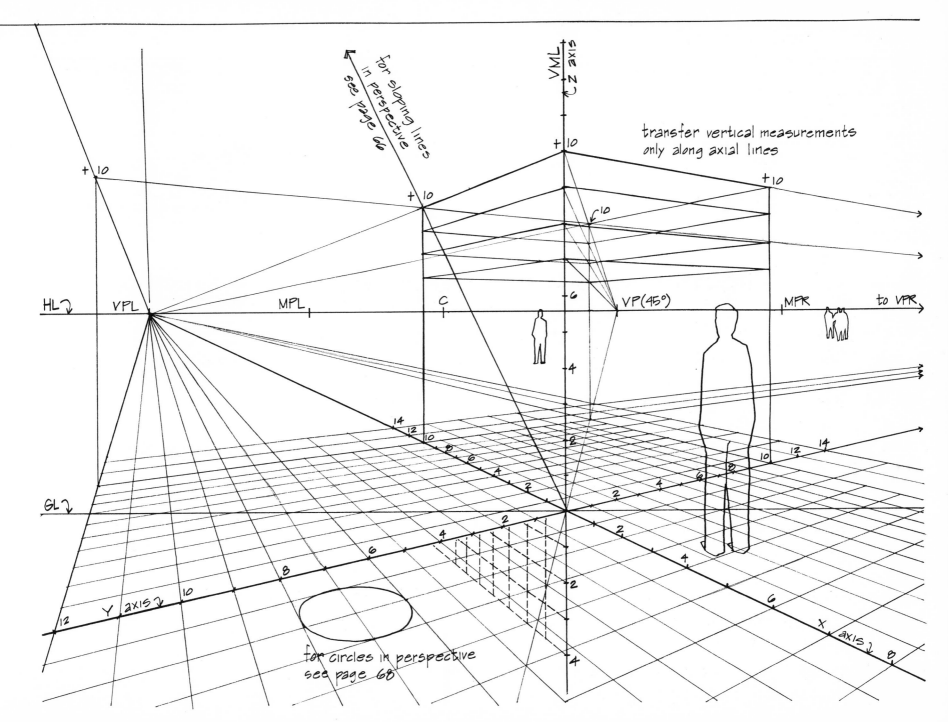

for sloping lines
in perspective
see page 66

VML
Z axis

transfer vertical measurements
only along axial lines

+10

+10

+10

+10

10

HL
VPL
MPL
C
VP (45°)
MFR
to VPR

6

4

14
12
10
8
6
4
2

2

8

2
4
6
8
10
12
14

GL

4

2

2

4

2

4

6
8
10
Y axis

12

6

X axis
0

for circles in perspective
see page 68

A sloping line in perspective can be determined by locating its ends in perspective and connecting these points in a manner similar to the drawing of nonaxonometric lines in a paraline drawing (see page 40). If, however, there are series of sloping lines in your design (stairs, ramps, sloping roofs, etc.) it would be useful to find their vanishing points.

To find the vanishing point for any sloping line:

① determine the vanishing point for a <u>horizontal</u> line which lies in the same <u>vertical</u> plane as the sloping line

② a vertical line through this vanishing point is the vanishing trace for the vertical plane

③ from the vanishing point found in ① scale off a distance along the horizon line equivalent to the distance from the station point to the vanishing point (from the plan setup)

④ from this point on the horizon line draw a line at the <u>true</u> slope of the sloping line

⑤ the point at which this sloping line intersects the vanishing trace is the vanishing point for the sloping line and all lines parallel to it

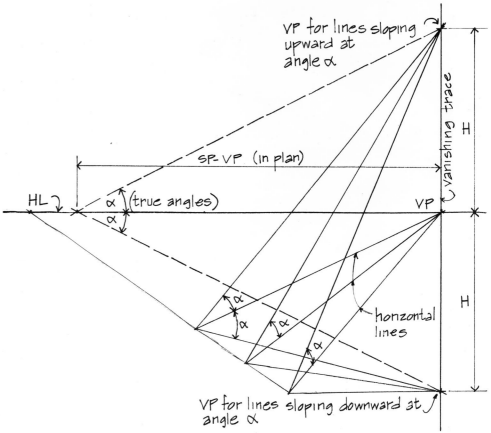

VP for lines sloping upward at angle α

vanishing trace

SP-VP (in plan)

H

HL

α (true angles)

α

VP

horizontal lines

H

VP for lines sloping downward at angle α

* note that if a set of parallel lines sloping upwards at angle α has its vanishing point H distance above the horizon line, a set of parallel lines sloping downward at an equal angle will have its vanishing point an identical distance below the horizon line

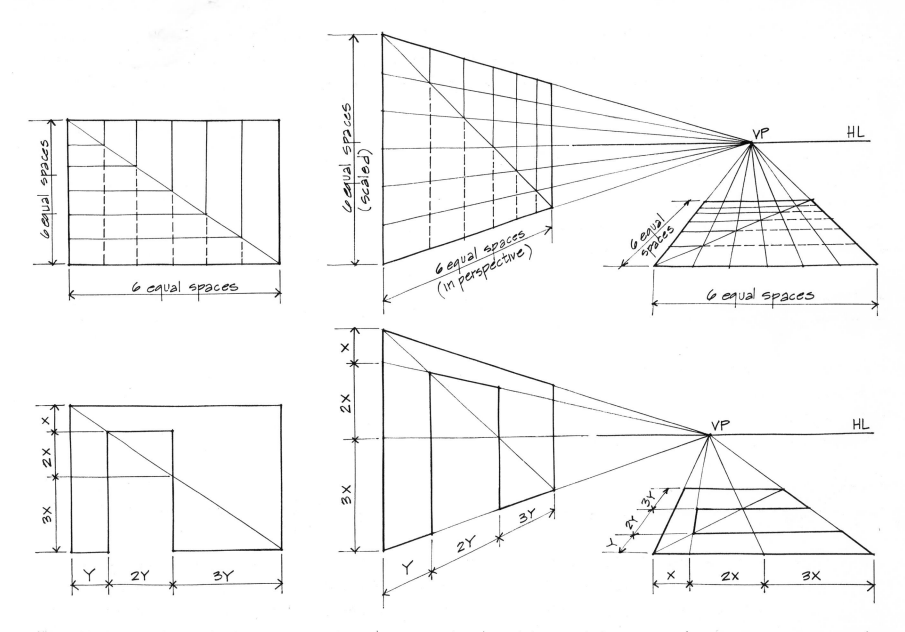

6 equal spaces

6 equal spaces

6 equal spaces (scaled)

6 equal spaces (in perspective)

6 equal spaces

6 equal spaces

VP   HL

X
2X
3X

Y   2Y   3Y

X
2X
3X

Y   2Y   3Y

Y 2Y 3Y

VP   HL

X   2X   3X

Diagonals can be used to conveniently divide vertical and horizontal rectangular planes in perspective into both equal and unequal segments.

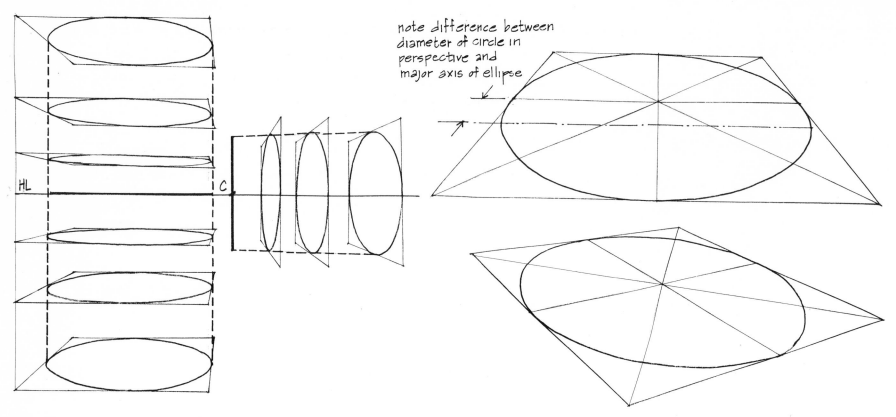

note difference between diameter of circle in perspective and major axis of ellipse

① circles <u>remain</u> circles in perspective when they are <u>parallel</u> to the picture plane

② when the plane of the circle is horizontal and lies at the same height as the observer, the circle appears as a horizontal line; when the plane of the circle is vertical and lies along the observer's line of sight perpendicular to the picture plane, the circle appears as a vertical line

③ in most other situations a circle appears as an approximate ellipse:

   • draw a square which circumscribes the circle in perspective
   • sketch in the circle as an approximate ellipse

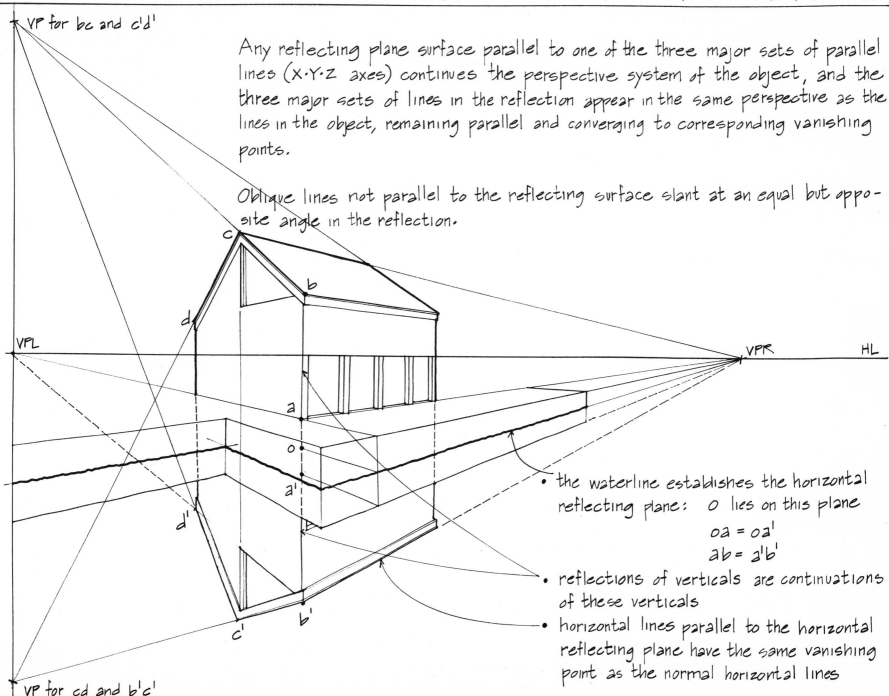

VP for bc and c'd'

Any reflecting plane surface parallel to one of the three major sets of parallel lines (X·Y·Z axes) continues the perspective system of the object, and the three major sets of lines in the reflection appear in the same perspective as the lines in the object, remaining parallel and converging to corresponding vanishing points.

Oblique lines not parallel to the reflecting surface slant at an equal but opposite angle in the reflection.

c

b

d

VPL

a

o

a'

VPR   HL

d'

• the waterline establishes the horizontal reflecting plane: O lies on this plane

$$oa = oa'$$
$$ab = a'b'$$

• reflections of verticals are continuations of these verticals

• horizontal lines parallel to the horizontal reflecting plane have the same vanishing point as the normal horizontal lines

c'   b'

VP for cd and b'c'

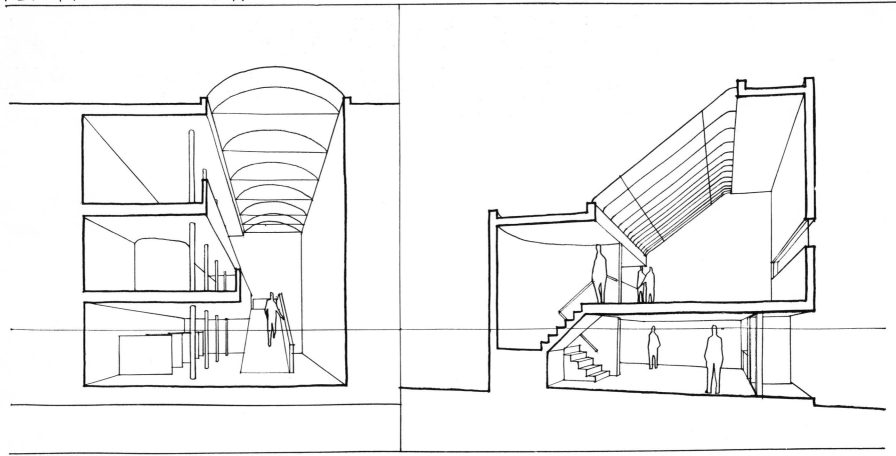

A building section (see pages 30-31) can also be seen in perspective (either one- or two-point), introducing a more natural, pictorial view of the spaces that are cut through while retaining the spatial relationships and definition that a building section normally illustrates.

In constructing a perspective section the vertical cutting plane of the section becomes the picture plane in perspective.

As with the building section, emphasis should be placed on the interior and exterior spaces that are cut through rather than the construction details within the structure itself.

RENDITION OF VALUE & CONTEXT

We derive meaning from a drawing through its figure-ground context, its positive and negative images, and the relationship between its light and dark areas.

In the last chapter a pure-line drawing technique was utilized. While contour drawings without value or tone can be quite elegant as two-dimensional graphic objects, they are only abstract images of reality and portray basically an outline world, a world without light.

In a contour drawing nonessentials are eliminated, and only those lines which indicate a change of form are emphasized. (Secondary lines may indicate changes in material.) Since we see an object first as a two-dimensional shape, its profile (outline or edge against space) is its most important aspect, and its profile line should therefore have the most weight.

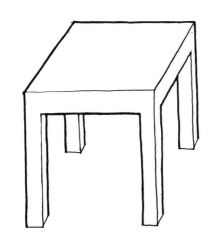

Plan, section, elevation, and paraline drawings done purely in line are dependent on line quality (clarity, consistency, continuity) and line-weight differentiation and hierarchy to express shape and spatial depth. Perspective line drawings can also use the conventions of overlapping forms, diminution of size, foreshortening, and convergence of parallel lines to portray the third dimension. Generally, however, pure-line drawings convey only limited information and almost always contain ambiguities.

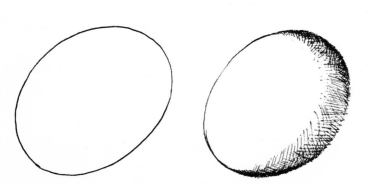

Although all drawing is representational and the difference between a pure-line drawing and a drawing utilizing tone is only one of degree of abstraction, a drawing with tonal value normally conveys more information about the object drawn. Living in a world of light, we find that a <u>change in tonal value is the basis for our perception of form.</u>

A blank piece of white paper is directionless, limitless, without dimension, infinite in depth. Once we place an area of value or tone on it, the sheet gains dimension and direction.

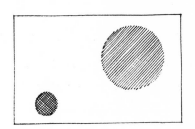

Two spots of equal area and intensity (degree of blackness) appear to lie in the same plane.

If the intensity of one is reduced, however, it usually appears to recede, while the darker one advances, due to its greater contrast with the white field. This change in value can communicate spatial depth visually.

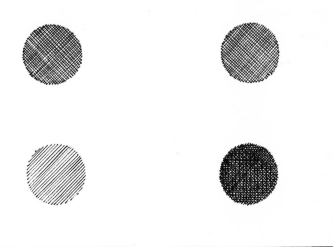

Likewise, two rectangles of equal line weight appear to be in the same plane. Again, as we increase the line weight of one, it appears to advance, while the other recedes.

If a change in tonal value is the basis for the perception of form, then <u>contrast</u> in value is the key to the graphic definition of form. This contrast must be <u>discernible</u>. In using tones or material renditions to depict form, you must be able to stand back from a drawing (or use a reducing glass) and judge visually whether or not sufficient contrast exists within the appropriate areas of the drawing to communicate the qualities of form and space you have in mind.

There are four basic techniques of drawing, which utilize different media to render form:

① pure-line drawing :   careful attention must be paid to line quality (clarity, consistency, continuity) and proper line-weight differentiation and hierarchy

  • cut lines
  • profile lines (silhouettes)
  • transitions in form (corners)
  • surface textures
  • material changes

② tone of lines
③ pure tone   whenever a tonal technique is employed, the discernible changes in value (through the rendition of materials, textures, shaded surfaces, and shadows) can by themselves imply the lines which normally define spatial edges and planar corners

④ line and tone   when changes in value are not rendered discernibly, the spatial edges and planar corners of a form must be reinforced by a line technique

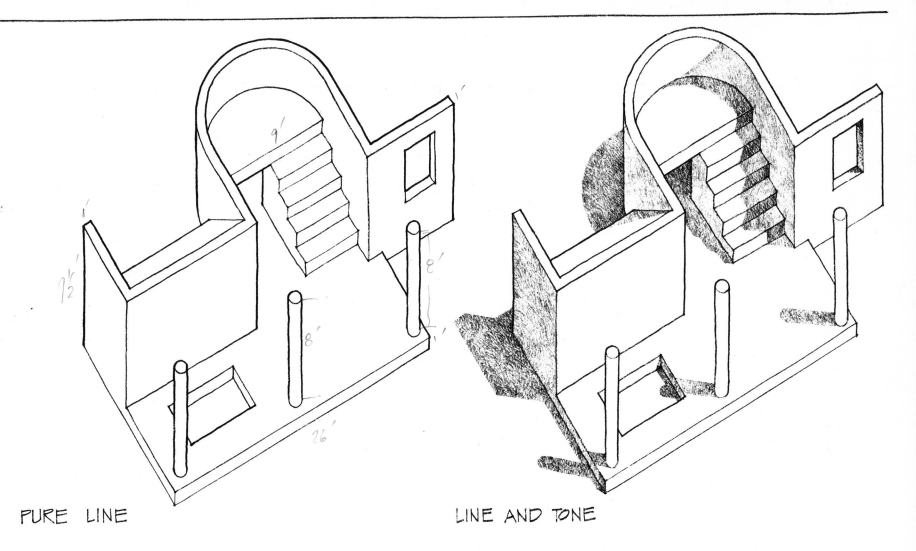

PURE LINE

- lines define spatial edges and planar corners
- a heavier line is used to profile (or silhouette) edges against space

LINE AND TONE

- lines define spatial edges and planar corners
- profiling is optional
- even tonal values render flat surfaces
- uneven tonal values indicate curvilinear forms
- shadows are generally darker than surfaces in shade

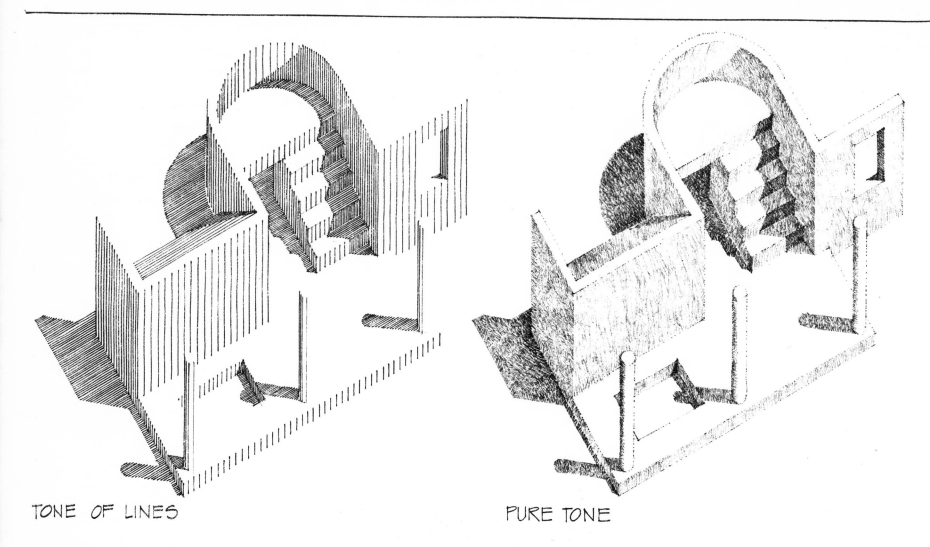

TONE OF LINES

PURE TONE

- changes in line spacing define spatial edges and planar corners (discernible change in value is mandatory)
- evenly spaced lines render flat planes
- unevenly spaced lines indicate curvilinear forms
- direction of lines should correspond to the vertical and horizontal orientation of the surfaces rendered

- changes in tonal value indicate spatial edges and planar corners
- changes in value must be discernible
- if tonal rendering has direction, this direction must correspond to the vertical and horizontal orientation of the surfaces

TECHNIQUE	MEDIA: BLACK AND WHITE		MEDIA: COLOR		PRINTS
• line • tone of lines	lead pencil black/gray ink black fiber-tip pen		colored pencil colored ink colored fiber-tip pen		blackline ozalid sepia ozalid Mylar ozalid photostat (negative and positive)
	line	**tone**	**line**	**tone**	
• line and tone	lead pencil fiber-tip pen ink	lead pencil Magic Marker Magic Marker ink wash Zip-a-Tone	pencil fiber-tip pen ink	pencil pastel Magic Marker Magic Marker watercolor wash Zip-a-Tone collage	above prints can be used as line-drawing bases for overlays
• pure tone	lead pencil charcoal ink wash Zip-a-Tone		color pencil pastel watercolor wash acrylic Zip-a-Tone		

On the facing page are four techniques for giving value and texture to a surface: all four are nondirectional except for lines used only in parallel. When lines are used only in parallel, the direction of those lines should reinforce the direction of the plane for which they are providing a value (ie. vertical lines for vertical planes / horizontal lines for horizontal planes).

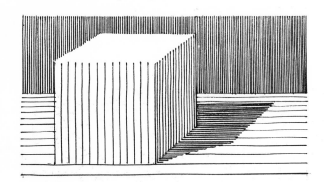
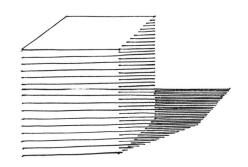
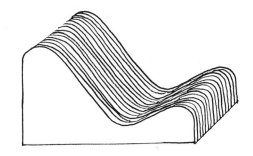

Between white and black exists a whole range of grays. None of the following four illustrations shows a smooth transition from white to black. In all of them, however, at a point between white and black the individual lines, scribbles, or dots lose their singular identity (not their identity as technique) and merge to form a field of gray. At this point there is sufficient contrast with a white field so that a line is not necessary to define the edge of the gray field. This should be remembered in the rendition of shades and shadows to avoid giving too much weight to the edge of a shade or shadow and allowing it to compete with the more important edge of a plane.

When giving a flat plane a surface value or texture, the rendition should be constant across the entire field of the plane. Lighter spots or subtle changes in value will cause the plane to appear warped.

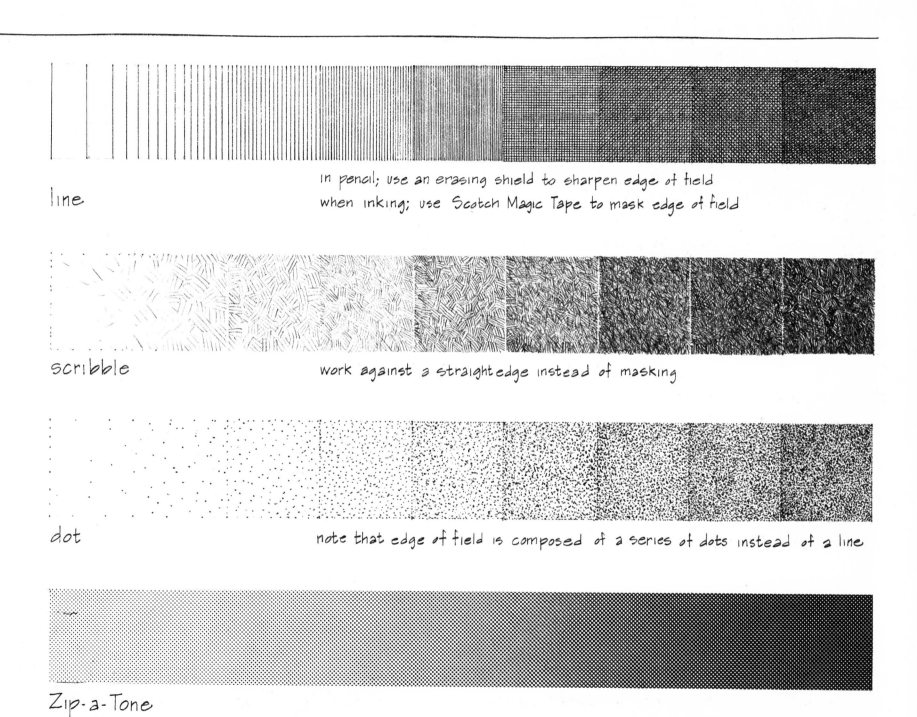

line

in pencil; use an erasing shield to sharpen edge of field
when inking; use Scotch Magic Tape to mask edge of field

scribble

work against a straight edge instead of masking

dot

note that edge of field is composed of a series of dots instead of a line

Zip-a-Tone

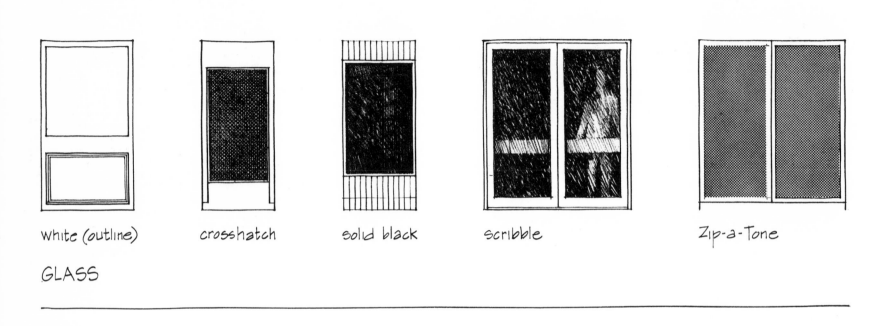

white (outline)   crosshatch   solid black   scribble   Zip-a-Tone

GLASS

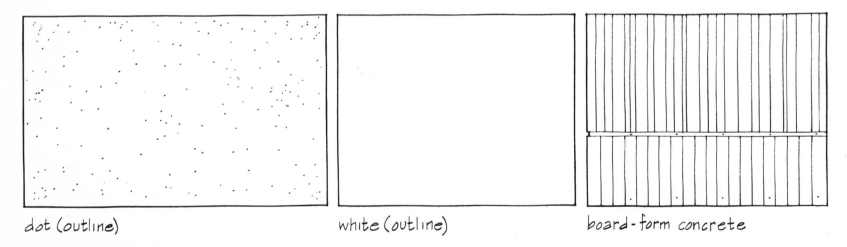

dot (outline)   white (outline)   board-form concrete

CONCRETE

plan

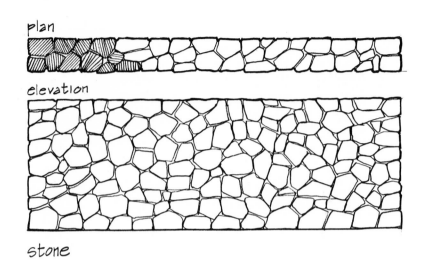

elevation

stone

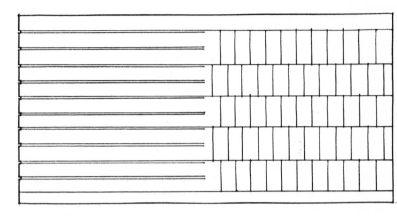

concrete block

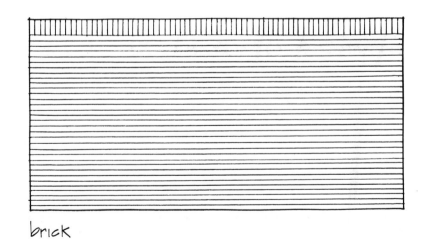

brick

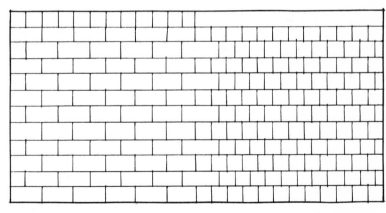

concrete block

MASONRY

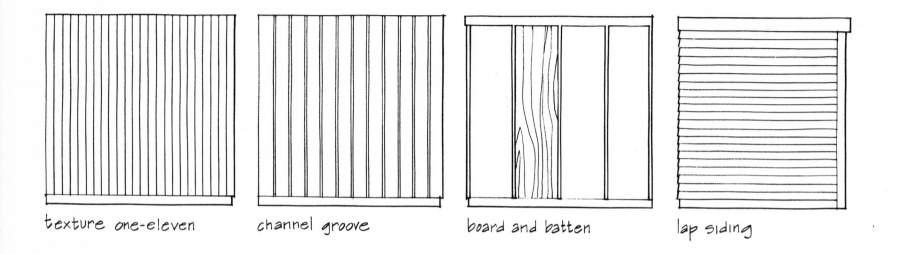

texture one-eleven   channel groove   board and batten   lap siding

paneling   random siding   diagonal siding

WOOD

82

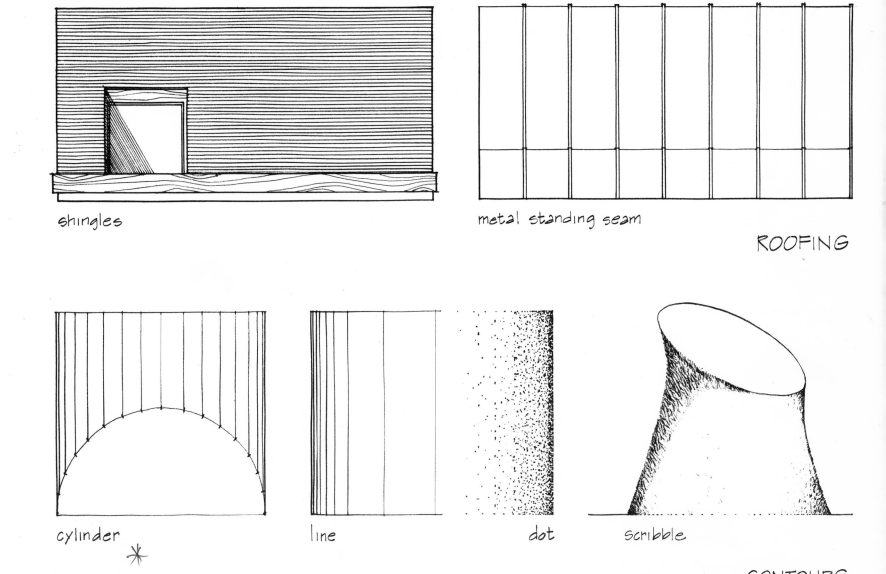

shingles

metal standing seam

cylinder

line

dot

scribble

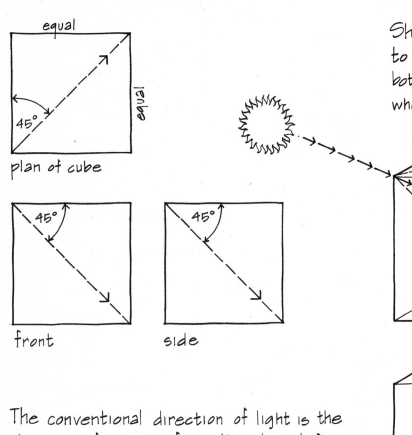

equal

45°

plan of cube

equal

45°

front

45°

side

Shades and shadows are used in architectural graphics to make drawings more easily understood by expressing both the third dimension of depth and the form of surfaces, whether flat or rounded, slanted or vertical.

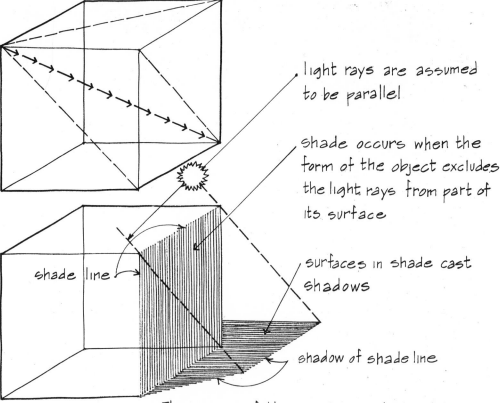

light rays are assumed to be parallel

shade occurs when the form of the object excludes the light rays from part of its surface

surfaces in shade cast shadows

shade line

shadow of shade line

The conventional direction of light is the diagonal of a cube from the top-left- (or right-) front corner to the bottom-right- (or left-) rear corner, so in plan and elevation views the direction of light is seen as the diagonal of a square.

This 45° direction of light results in shadows of widths equal to the projections from wall surfaces of vertical and horizontal shade lines.

The shape of the shadow is dependent on:
- the position of the shade line
- the position of the observer
- the direction of light
- the form of the surface on which the plane of the shadow falls

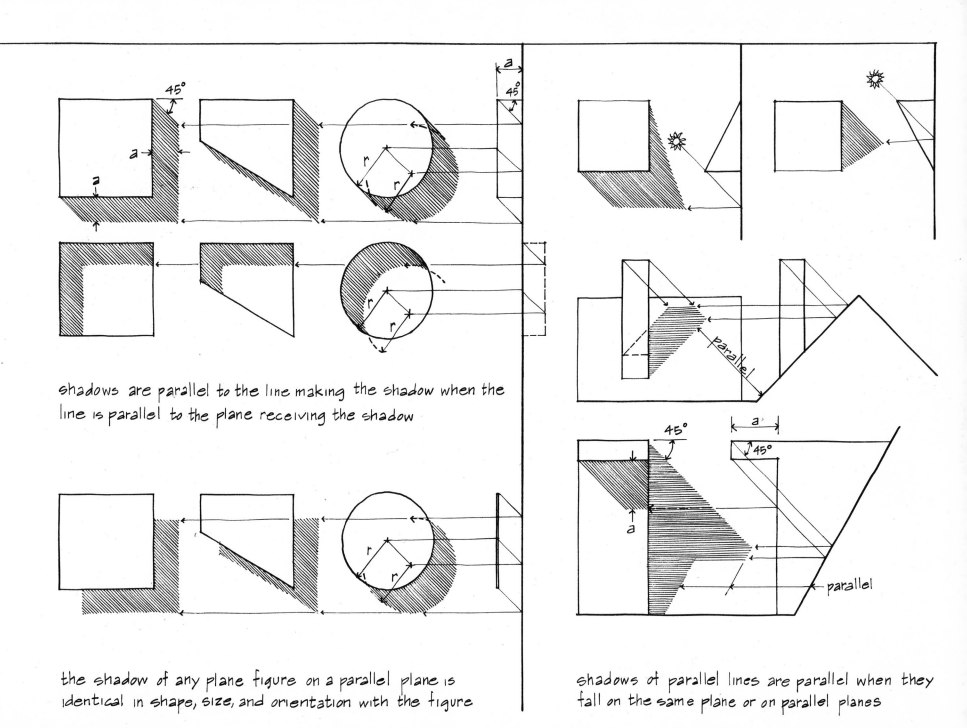

shadows are parallel to the line making the shadow when the line is parallel to the plane receiving the shadow

the shadow of any plane figure on a parallel plane is identical in shape, size, and orientation with the figure

shadows of parallel lines are parallel when they fall on the same plane or on parallel planes

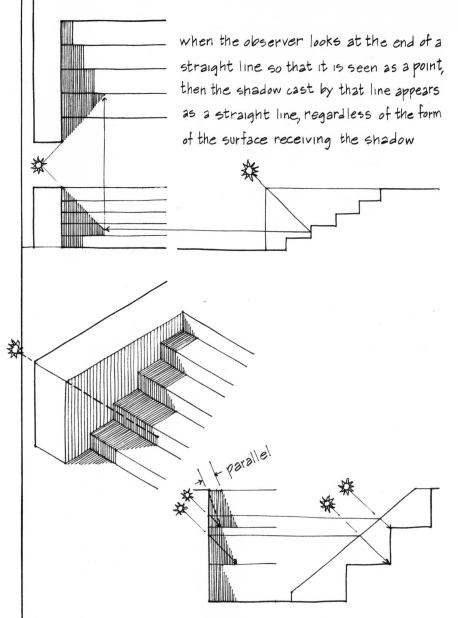

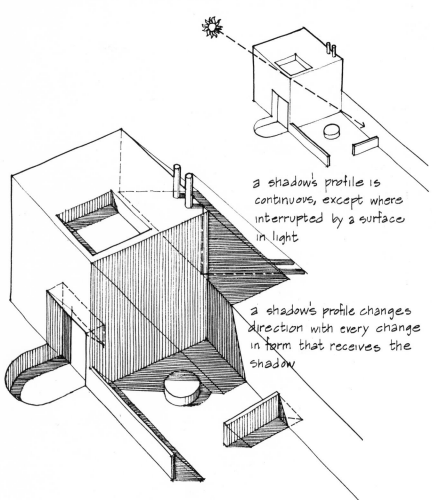

when the observer looks at the end of a
straight line so that it is seen as a point,
then the shadow cast by that line appears
as a straight line, regardless of the form
of the surface receiving the shadow

a shadow's profile is
continuous, except where
interrupted by a surface
in light

a shadow's profile changes
direction with every change
in form that receives the
shadow

to determine the shadow cast by a complex form:

① break down the complex form into its simplest
geometric components
② determine the shadows cast by these components
③ the overall shadow pattern will be a composite of
these shadows

parallel

the shadow of any straight line on a plane surface can be
located by finding the shadows of the ends of that line

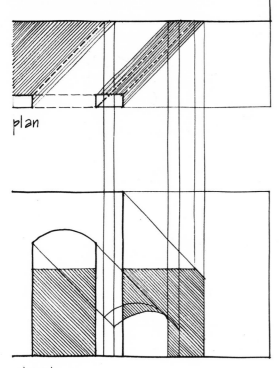

plan

elevation

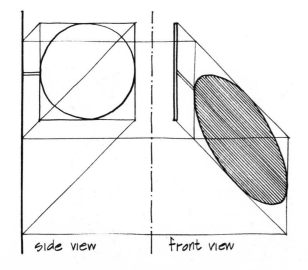

side view front view

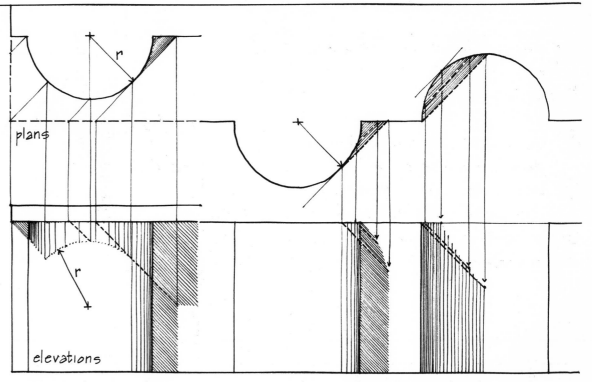

plans

r

r

elevations

shadows of curved lines can be determined by 45° projections of critical points (0°, 45°, 90°, 135°)

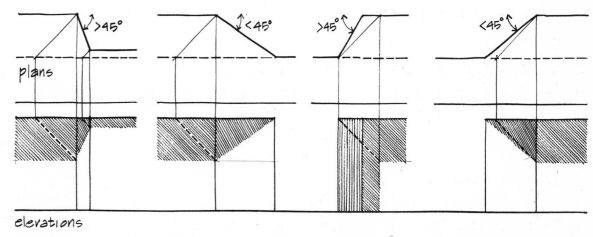

>45° <45° >45° <45°

plans

elevations

The purpose of shades and shadows in the rendition of site plans is threefold:

① to indicate the height of masses above the ground plane
② to provide a contrast in value to emphasize the building form
③ to indicate significant changes in topography

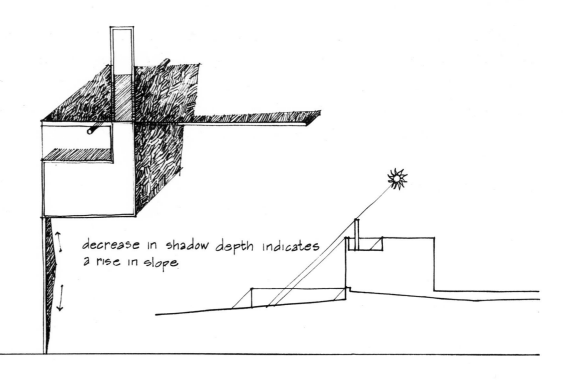

decrease in shadow depth indicates a rise in slope

In addition to using a flat or slightly textured (line, dot, or scribble) field of gray to indicate shades and shadows, an alternate method of intensifying a material-rendition pattern can be utilized to indicate the shade and/or shadow without losing a sense of what sort of material is in shade or receiving the shadow.

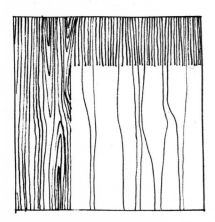
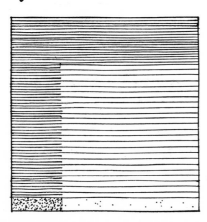
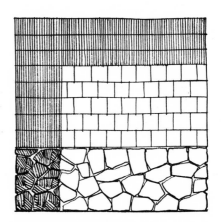
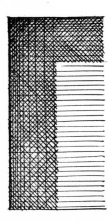

In the discussion of the three major types of architectural drawing in chapter 3, you were encouraged to illustrate architecture in its context. This inclusion of the physical environs was done primarily by extending the ground line or plane and indicating the adjacent form, whether natural topography or construction. The importance of providing context in architectural drawings lies in the need to design and evaluate architecture in relationship to its environment, whether urban or rural, old or new.

The purpose of this section is to enable you to indicate as clearly as possible, without obscuring the focus on architecture, not only the physical but also the human context, and in so doing to indicate also the scale and use of the spaces depicted.

The following contextual devices will be illustrated: people
 furniture
 cars
 landscaping

In order not to obscure the purpose of an architectural drawing:

① use only those contextual devices necessary to communicate context, scale, and usage
② draw contextual devices simply, with a minimum of detail
③ never obscure structural and space-defining elements and their relationships
④ the size, weight (value), and placement of contextual devices must be seen as important elements in a drawing's overall composition

The viewer of a drawing relates to the human figures within it; he becomes one of them and thus is drawn into the scene.

- the purpose of placing human figures in an architectural drawing is to indicate scale

- the placement of human figures can indicate spatial depth and levels

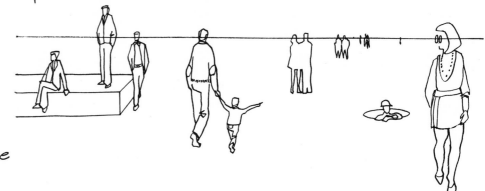

- the number, disposition, and dress of human figures can indicate usage of a space

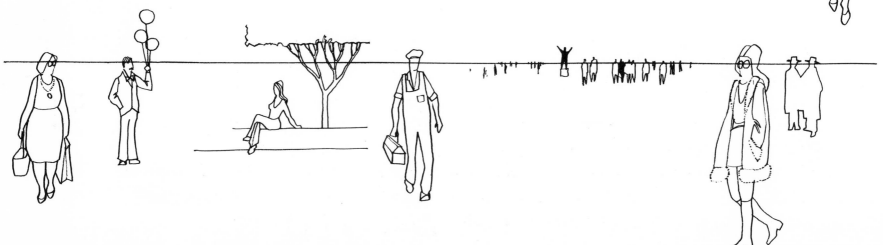

The important features of human figures, aside from their disposition, are:

- proportion
- size
- attitude

The human figure can be broken down into seven equal parts; the head is one-seventh of the total body height.

It is generally easiest to start human figures with the head at eye level. In orthographic and paraline drawings the 5'-6' height can be scaled. In perspectives the horizon line is at the viewer's eye level, so we can start at the horizon line. Figures above or below the level of the viewer can first be sized as if on the same level and then shifted up or down as required.

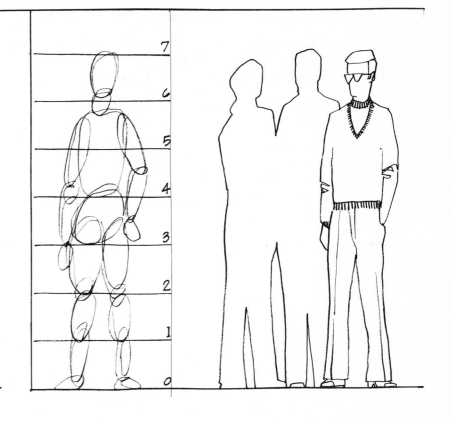

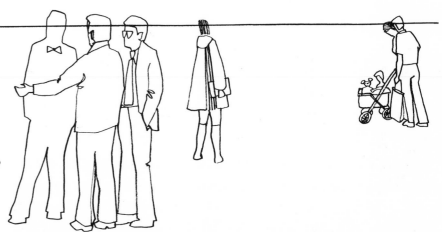

- indicate activity appropriate to the space
- avoid stiff, upright figures and hyperactive groups
- in composition, utilize both groups and solitary figures that are consistent with the usage of the space

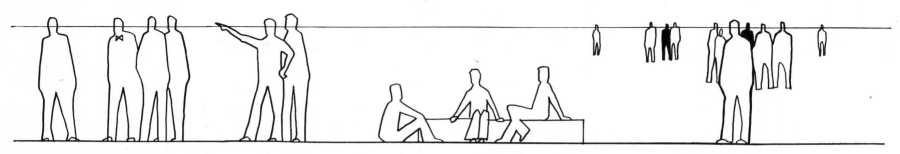

Figures can be abstractly outlined for use in a pure-line drawing with shades of gray so as not to detract from the focus on the architecture, or they can be given some detail that is consistent with the scale, composition, and style of the drawing.

It is a good practice to collect and compile a file of magazine and newspaper photographs of people and their activities to provide tracers for various situations.

Be consistent: each one of us inevitably develops his or her own style of drawing.

drawing furniture in conjunction with people helps to keep them in scale

keep furniture simple in plan

Be realistic with the placement - to indicate roadways and parking areas
            and the scale - drawing cars in conjunction with people helps to keep them in scale.

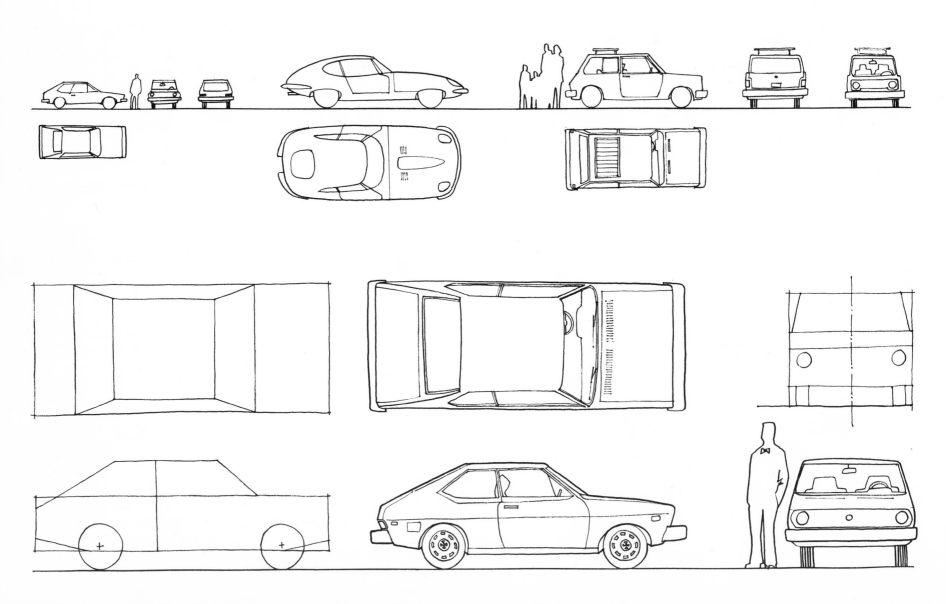

95

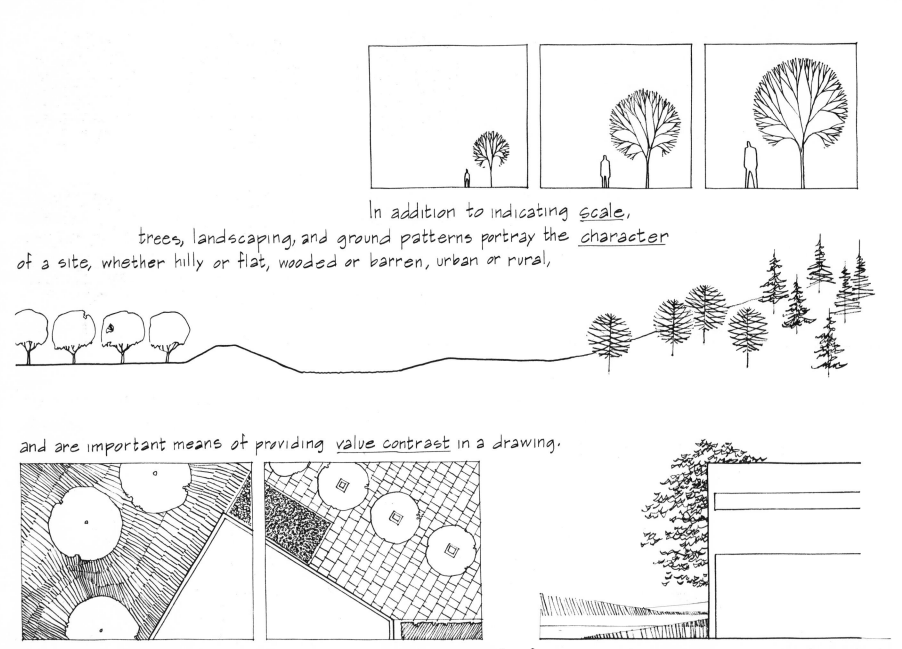

In addition to indicating <u>scale</u>, trees, landscaping, and ground patterns portray the <u>character</u> of a site, whether hilly or flat, wooded or barren, urban or rural,

and are important means of providing <u>value contrast</u> in a drawing.

entourage should never compete with but rather act as a foil for the architecture that is being illustrated

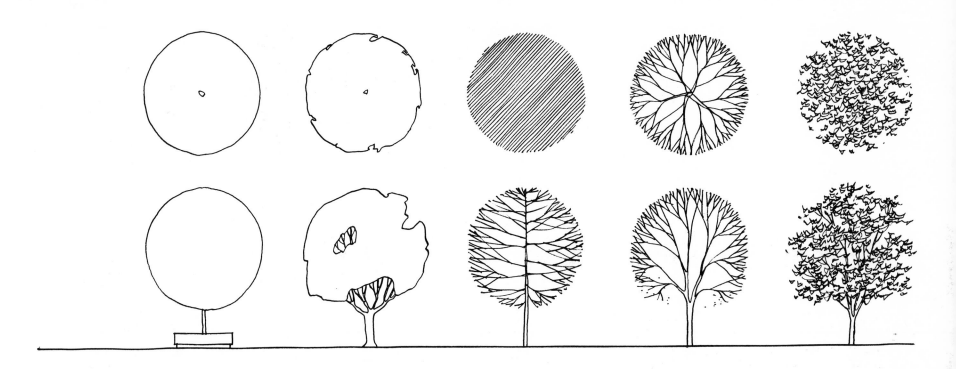

Be economical. The style of an architectural drawing should be consistent throughout: freehand entourage in a freehand drawing; hard-line entourage (abstracted as required) in a hard-line drawing. The amount of detail rendered should be consistent with the scale of the drawing.

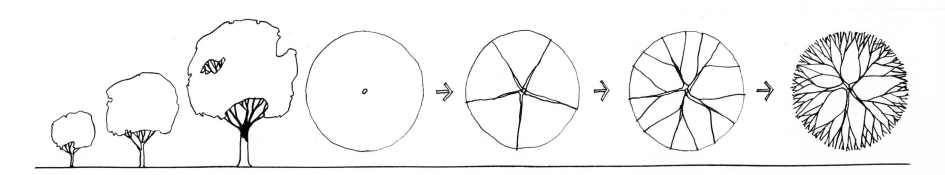

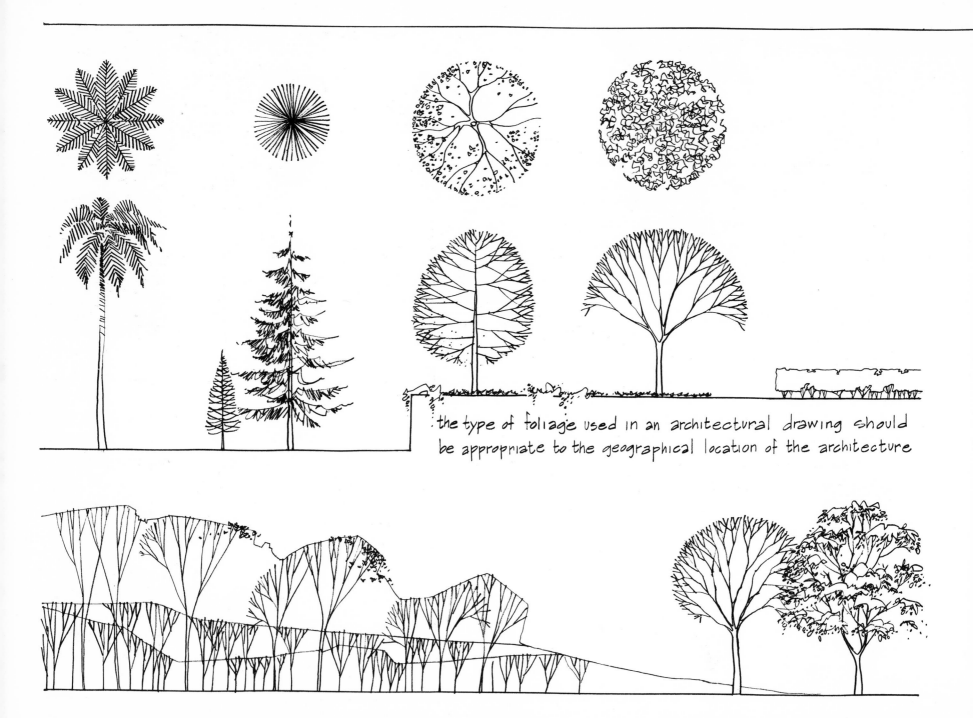

the type of foliage used in an architectural drawing should
be appropriate to the geographical location of the architecture

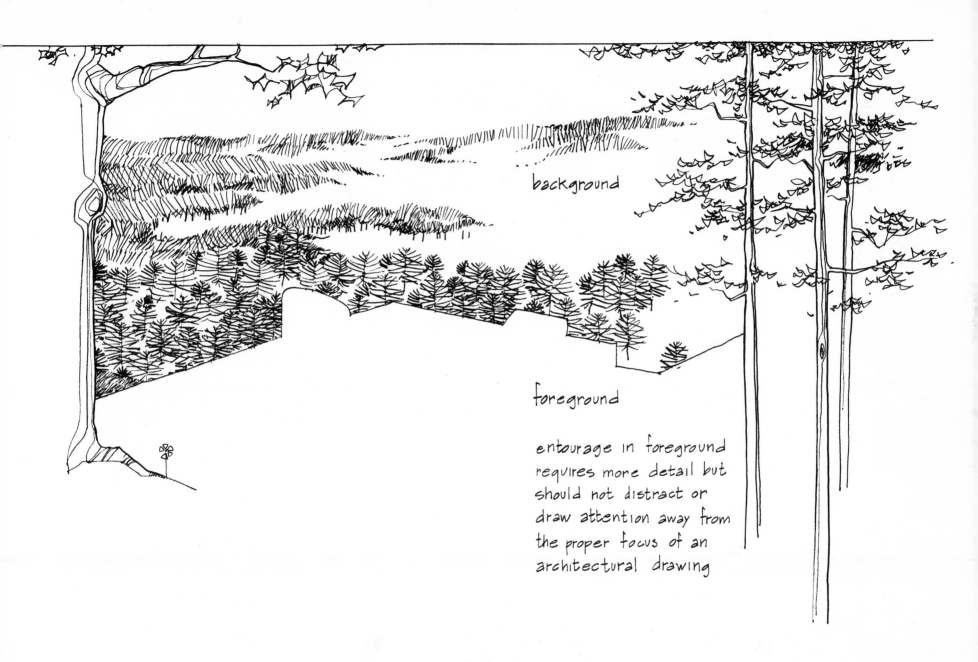

background

foreground

entourage in foreground
requires more detail but
should not distract or
draw attention away from
the proper focus of an
architectural drawing

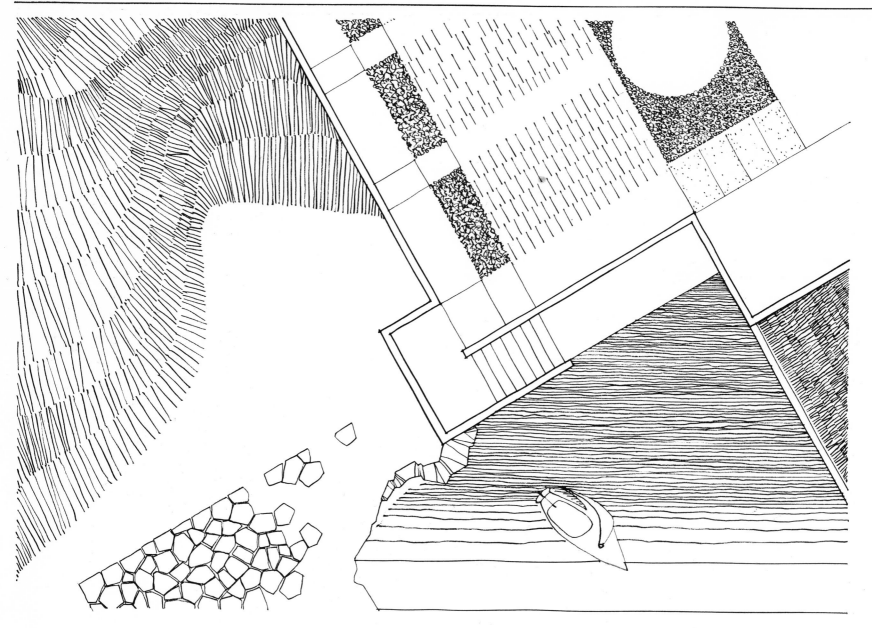

The value (grayness) of a ground-plane texture should provide the degree of contrast required to define the appropriate relationship between adjacent forms.

Everything which appears in front of or above a reflecting surface (glass, water, plastic, etc.) appears in back of or below the reflecting surface in a direction perpendicular to the surface (vertically or toward a vanishing point). Objects appear at the same distance in back of or below the reflecting surface as they do in front of or above that surface (see page 60).

Water should be rendered as a <u>horizontal</u> planar surface. Use essentially <u>horizontal</u> lines - drafted for still water; freehand, wavy lines for ripply water.

Surfaces that are light in value appear lighter than the value of the water. Likewise, darker surfaces appear darker in reflection than the value of the water's surface.

GRAPHIC SYMBOLS & LETTERING

This chapter discusses graphic symbols and lettering, which help the viewer to identify and orient himself to the various architectural drawing elements that comprise a presentation. In enhancing the clarity and readability of architectural drawings, these devices become important elements in the overall composition of a presentation.

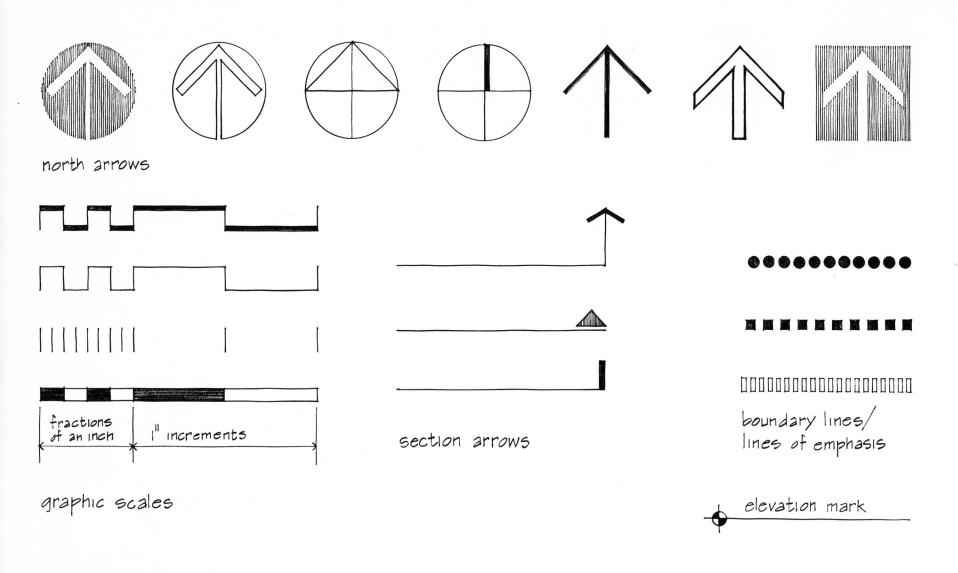

north arrows

graphic scales

fractions of an inch | 1" increments

section arrows

boundary lines/ lines of emphasis

elevation mark

Graphic presentation symbols are conventions, which rely on their graphic images to convey information. To be easily recognizable and readable, these images should be kept simple and clean (ie. free of extraneous stylization).

All graphic presentation symbols and lettering must be considered elements in the composition of a presentation. Their impact on the composition is dependent on their size, weight, and placement.

size   should be determined on the basis of:

              ① readability from the observer's point of view
              ② the proportional relationship of the graphic symbols or lettering to the overall size and scale of the drawing

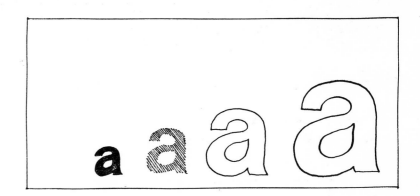

weight   is determined by the size and value (ranging from white through a series of grays to black) of the graphic symbols or letters, i.e., if a large-sized typeface is required for readability from a certain distance, but a low value is mandatory for a balanced composition, then an outline letter should be used

placement   of titles and graphic symbols should be determined on the basis of their overall weight or tonal value and their role in the organization of the presentation

ABCDEFGHIJKLMNOPQRRSTUVWXYZ   1234567890
ABCDEFGHIJKLMNOPQRRSTUVWXYZ   1234567890

The use of guidelines is mandatory for letters to be consistent in height.

For letters to communicate and not to distract or detract from the drawing itself:

① keep lettering vertical
a small triangle is a quick
and efficient way to keep
vertical lettering strokes
consistently vertical

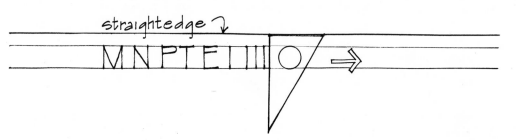

slanted lettering is directional; this movement is generally distracting in a rectilinear drawing scheme

② maintain oblong proportions for the most stable lettering

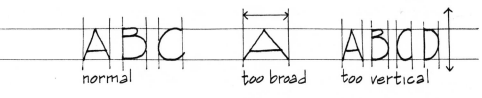

normal   too broad   too vertical

Everyone inevitably develops an individual style of lettering. The most important characteristics of a lettering style are: readability and consistency, in both style and spacing.

Letter spacing is not based on equal spacing between the extremeties of the letters but on equal areas.

equal areas
correct

equal spacing
incorrect

lower-case lettering can be appropriate if it is sympathetic to the drawing style and if it is executed consistently throughout the presentation. It is generally easy to read, because we recognize the distinctive differences among the characters from its widespread use in the printing industry.

abcdefgghijklmnopqrstuvwxyz

SERIFS enhance the recognition and readability of an alphabet. They too should be used consistently. Perhaps the best example of the use of serifs is the classic roman alphabet, which is the model for the single-stroke alphabet below:

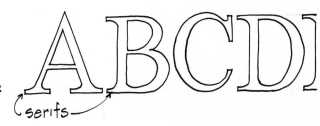
serifs

ABCDEFGHIJKLMNOPQRSTUVWXYZ · 1234567890

The maximum-sized single-stroke letter or numeral that should be used is 3/16". Beyond this size a letter or numeral should have width and substance to its strokes so it doesn't appear too weak.

With the wealth of well-designed alphabets and typefaces available, you should not spend time designing new ones but rather learn when and where to utilize the existing ones. For this purpose, a press-on lettering catalog is excellent source material.

The character of the typeface used in the verbal supplement to the graphic presentation should be appropriate to the architecture being presented. The typeface can be consistent with the architectural style, or it can act as a foil or counterpoint to the subject matter.

The following page shows some representative typefaces.

helvetica medium is a relatively neutral, well-proportioned alphabet; other sans serif (without serifs) alphabets are:

- folio medium
- standard medium
- univers 53
- venus medium

lighter in weight and more elegant in character are:

- folio light
- helvetica light
- microgramma medium extended
- copperplate gothic
- optima stempel

a few sans serif alphabets with relatively heavy weight are:

- folio bold
- helvetica bold
- microgramma bold extended
- univers 75

similar in weight but with serifs are:

- clarendon bold
- fortune bold (and extra bold)
- windsor bold

ABCDEFGHIJKLMNOPQRSTUVWXYZ 1234567890

FREEHAND DRAWING

This chapter first discusses the technique of sketching from real life, an invaluable exercise which enables you to develop the skill to portray a condition or idea graphically quickly and accurately and at the same time forces you to observe and analyze your environment. The second part discusses the use of graphic diagraming in the design process as an important communication device for the designer.

FREEHAND SKETCHING

As a beginning student you should whenever possible take the opportunity to sketch from real life to develop your drawing skills and sharpen your awareness of the existing environment. While sketching, you should not concentrate merely on drawing technique, or you will lose sight of what you see. Sketching from life trains you to observe, analyze, and evaluate while recording your environment.

The subject matter that you record should range in scale from the general to the specific. You should look at how pieces of the environment fit together; how the built environment relates to the natural; how elements of the environment juxtapose themselves; how buildings define exterior space, frame vistas, form walls or horizontal planes; how some buildings are in fact objects in space, while others form backgrounds for various elements. Of course, you are always concerned with form, light, texture, and space.

Look at individual buildings. Why do some have character and others do not? Investigate the physical elements that make up buildings. Look at details: how doors and windows are constructed, how brick walls turn corners, how various materials meet.

Observation and investigation, properly evaluated, help to build up your vocabulary of the environment, which will serve as a basis for much of what you do in the design studio.

The finished sketch should communicate your observations and your point of view. Just as your hand should be able to record your observations graphically quickly and accurately, your eye should be able to grasp quickly and accurately the nature of those observations. Beginning students often have difficulty in sketching accurately, since they believe they can comprehend without careful observation, confusing psychological impressions in the mind with what they really see. Although the merits of impressionistic sketches are arguable, when the accuracy of a sketch deteriorates to the point of being incomprehensible to the viewer, the communicative power of the graphics is lost.

A variety of drawing instruments is available to the sketcher. At the start, you are encouraged to try all of the following: a soft pencil, HB or softer; a fountain pen with black ink; a black fiber-tip pen; a charcoal pencil; black and gray Magic Markers.

Experiment with the feel of each of these on various types of paper. Try to determine the limits of expression each is capable of and how its characteristics affect the nature of a sketch. For example, you should find that with a fine point you are capable of executing a variety of line types and further, that a pen-and-ink drawing consists mainly of lines. On the other hand, with a soft pencil or charcoal, you should be able to execute softer, more subtle lines and tones.

It should be noted that the width of a line (as determined by the drawing instrument you are using) determines how abstract or detailed a sketch can be. Drawing with a fine-point fountain pen encourages you to sketch in minute details. Since it takes innumerable fine ink lines to cover a given area, many fine ink-line drawings end up smaller than intended or, if large in size, weak in intensity. On the other hand, sketching with a Magic Marker forces you to look at and record broader lines and to eliminate details.

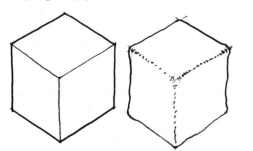

Sketches can consist purely of lines, or they can be combinations of line and tone, but the line remains the single most essential drawing element, since it is capable of such a wide range of expression. It can define shape and form and even imply a sense of depth and space. A line can portray hard as well as soft materials; it can be light or heavy, limp or taut, bold or tentative.

The following are examples of sketches, ranging in scale, subject matter, and technique.

a knowledge of the principles of perspective is
indispensable for the sketching of architectural forms

although a line drawing can be informative,
a sketch can also have tonal and textural interest

GRAPHIC DIAGRAMING

Graphic diagrams, because of the visual thinking they stimulate, are an important tool of the designer. Graphic diagrams are visual abstractions which depict the essence of :

    ① concepts (ideas, processes, events)
    ② objects   (physical elements varying in scale)

The act of diagraming various aspects of an architectural idea enables a designer to investigate and communicate at a very general level the overall organization of a scheme, both two-dimensionally and three-dimensionally. A graphic portrayal of a building's organization through diagrams can be helpful not only in enhancing and keying the viewer's understanding of the normal architectural presentation drawings but also in enabling the designer to keep sight of his original intent during the design process. An excellent and clear concept is often obscured if not destroyed in the process of a design proposal's refinement and resolution in detail.

Some of the aspects of a building which can be effectively diagramed are:

    ① functional zoning (horizontal and vertical)
    ② zoning of degrees of privacy
    ③ circulation (horizontal and vertical)
    ④ site conditions and context
    ⑤ spatial hierarchy and relationships
    ⑥ geometric properties
    ⑦ lighting conditions (natural and artificial)
    ⑧ structure and enclosure

There are others, of course. It should be remembered that two-dimensional diagrams can communicate not only organizational ideas but also the implications of form.

Technique and media can vary from very loose, amorphous, freehand sketches (doodles) to precise, hardline images.

Your choice of drawing equipment depends on the scale, the degree of abstraction, and the amount of detail.

In working from the general to the particular, from broad, overriding issues to a problem's resolution in detail, you are involved in abstraction, in separating the essential matter from more superficial concerns. Paralleling the gradual formulation, refinement, and crystallization of a problem (and the corresponding synthesis of given information and feedback), graphic technique progresses from generalized sketches, executed in broad strokes, to more definitive symbols of concrete ideas and solutions, executed with more precise instruments.

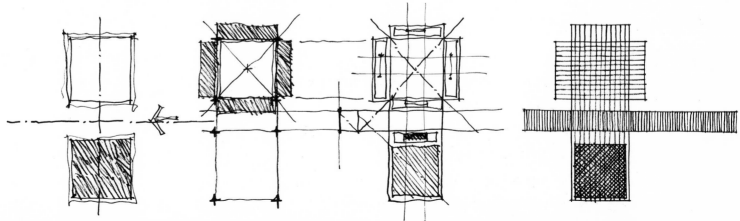

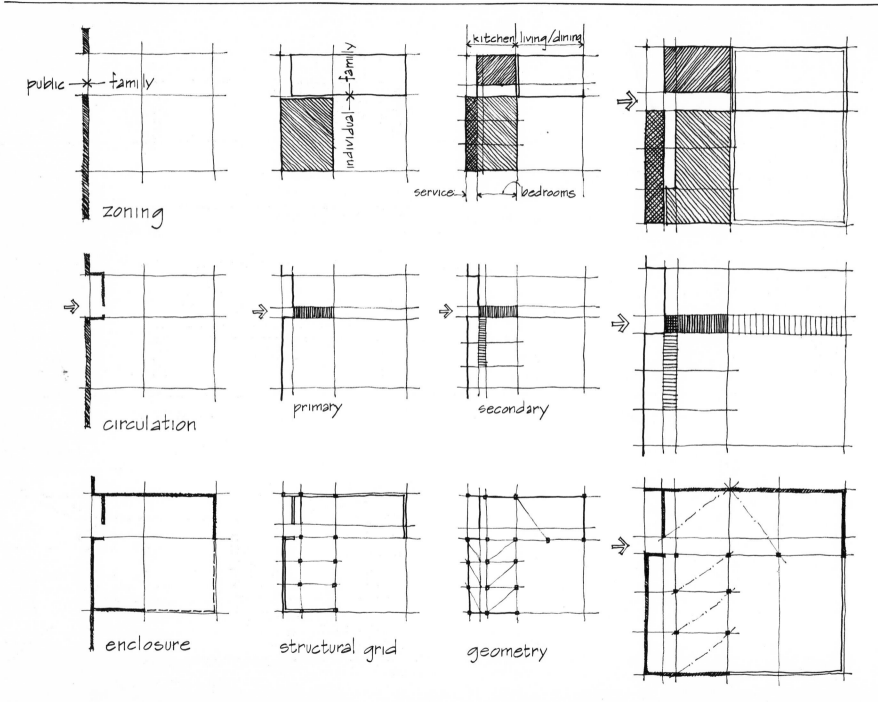

public —✕— family

zoning

kitchen living/dining

service —✕— bedrooms

family ✕ individual

circulation

primary

secondary

enclosure

structural grid

geometry

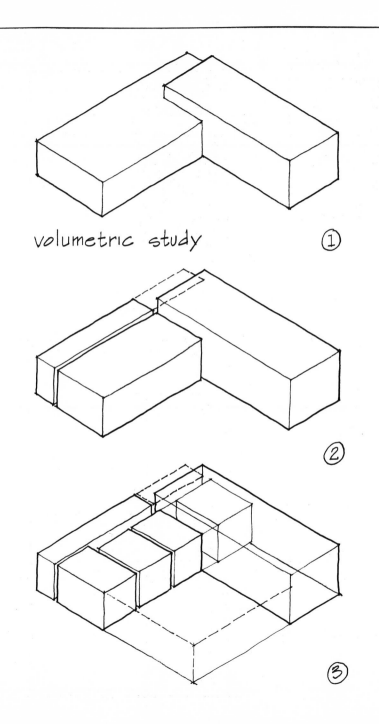

volumetric study   ①

②

③

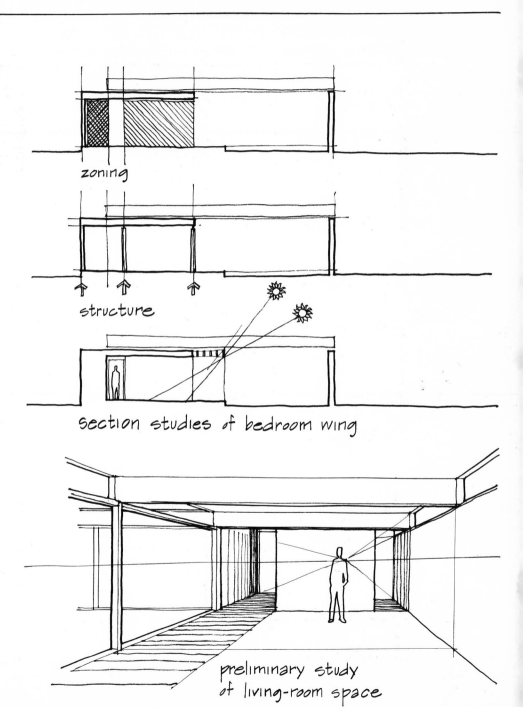

zoning

structure

section studies of bedroom wing

preliminary study
of living-room space

A well-developed ability to sketch enables a designer to investigate a number of alternatives quickly, accurately, and efficiently. With a roll of inexpensive yellow tracing paper and a soft pencil or marker, you should be able to start with a basic idea or scheme and, by a series of overlays and transformations, arrive at a number of reasonable alternatives. Every drawing or sketch along the way, whether the ideas it represents are accepted or rejected, helps you to gain further insight into the problem and often generates new ideas while enhancing the chances of cross-fertilization among any number of previous ideas.

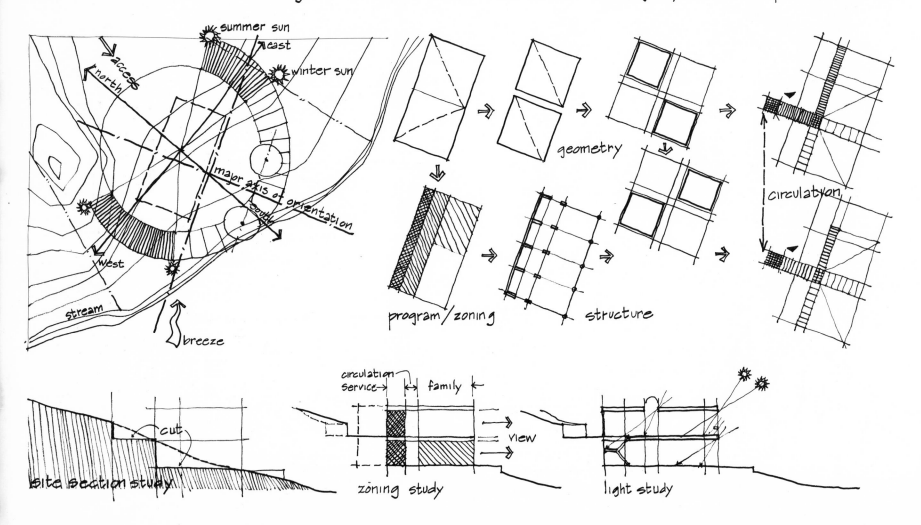

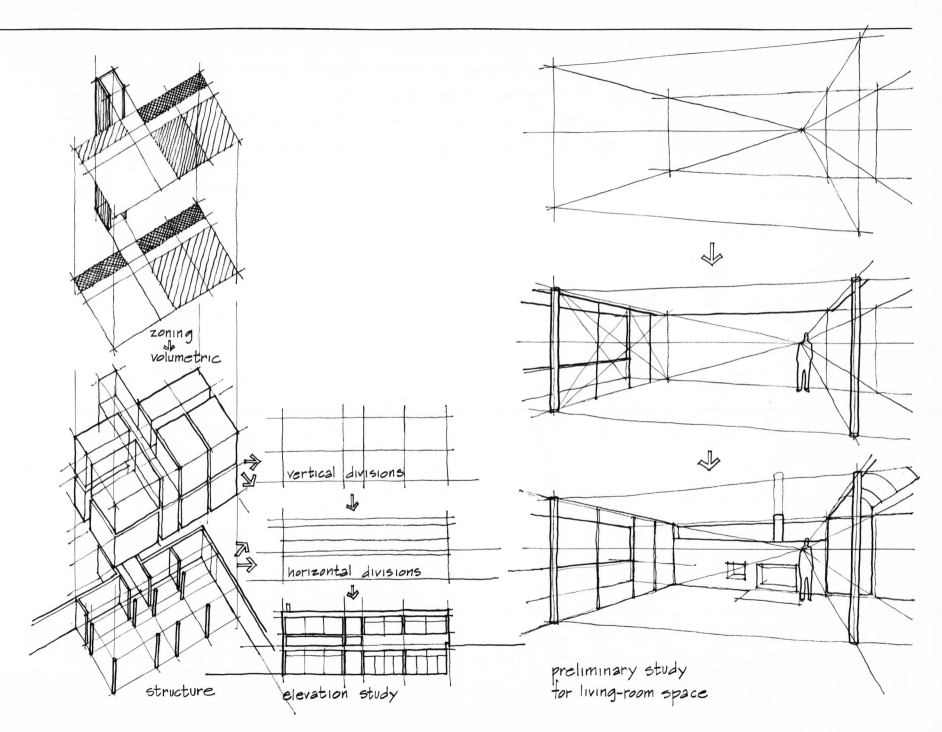

zoning
⇩
volumetric

structure

vertical divisions
⇩
horizontal divisions
⇩

elevation study

preliminary study
for living-room space

7 ARCHITECTURAL PRESENTATIONS

The primary purpose of architectural graphics is communication. Although the drawings that comprise an architectural presentation may be excellent two-dimensional graphics worthy of an exhibition, they are merely communicative tools, never primary ends in themselves.

An architectural presentation's drawings are its primary meanings of communication. Unless the architectural drawings and graphics are comprehensible – their conventions understood and their substance meaningful – the presentation will be weak and ineffective. An effective presentation, however, also possesses collective characteristics, which can enhance the readability of the drawings themselves:

① a point of view : a presentation should communicate the central idea of a design scheme – graphic diagrams/ abstractions/ overlays are effective means of articulating the various aspects of a design scheme, especially when they are visually related to the more common architectural drawings

② unity : in an effective presentation no one segment is inconsistent with or detracts from the whole
unity (not to be confused with uniformity) depends on:

- a logical and comprehensible arrangement of integrated graphic and verbal information
- a consistent scale/format/medium/technique synthesis appropriate to the design as well as to the place and audience for which the presentation is intended

③ continuity : each segment of a presentation should relate to what precedes and what follows it, reinforcing all the other segments of the presentation

The principles of unity and continuity are mutually self-supporting; one cannot be achieved without the other; the factors which produce one invariably reinforce the other. At the same time, however, emphasis on your central idea can be brought into focus through the placement and pacing of the major and supporting graphic and verbal elements which comprise the presentation.

④ efficiency: an effective presentation employs economy of means, utilizing only what is necessary to communicate an idea; if the graphic elements of a presentation become overly demonstrative and ends in themselves, the intent and purpose of the presentation are obscured

The composition and arrangement of the following elements must be considered in any architectural presentation:

- graphic images: architectural drawings
                                 graphic diagrams
- graphic/verbal information: north arrows, graphic scales, etc.
                                 titles, legends, etc.
- field/ground relationship: white/gray/colored residual spaces

All of these elements have the following properties, which must be considered in composing a visually balanced presentation:

- shape
- size   } weight
- value
- placement: direction/attitude/interval

Architectural presentations generally read from left to right and from top to bottom, except in the case of a slide presentation, where a sequence in time is primarily involved. The subject matter presented should progress from the general or contextual view to the specific, as illustrated on the following page.

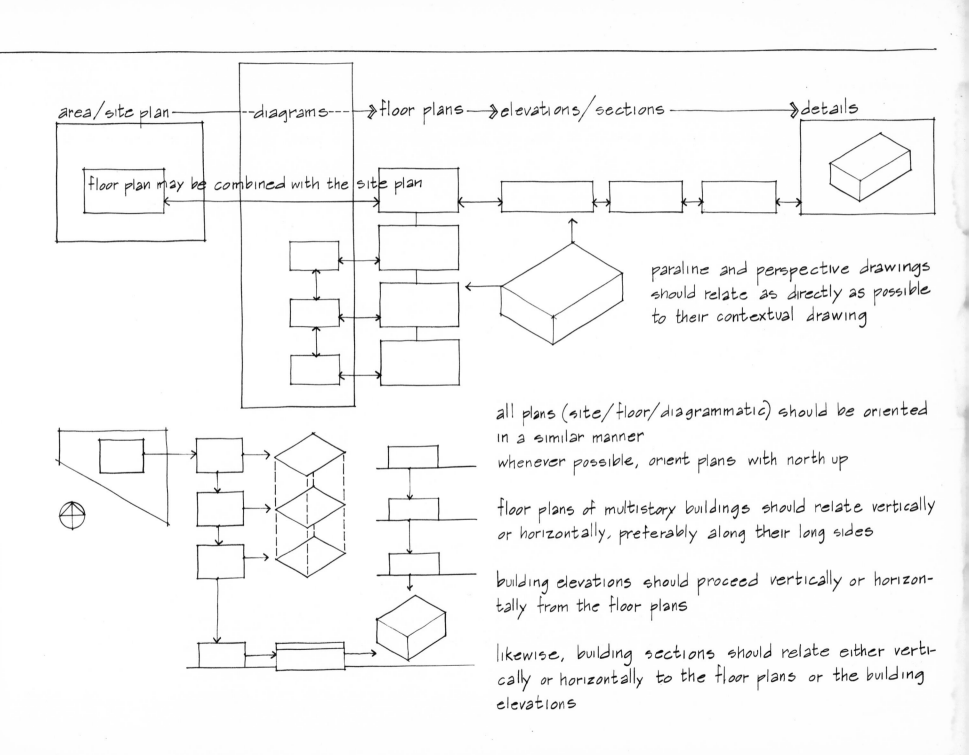

area/site plan———————---diagrams---->floor plans———->elevations/sections——————————————————>details

floor plan may be combined with the site plan

paraline and perspective drawings
should relate as directly as possible
to their contextual drawing

all plans (site/floor/diagrammatic) should be oriented
in a similar manner
whenever possible, orient plans with north up

floor plans of multistory buildings should relate vertically
or horizontally, preferably along their long sides

building elevations should proceed vertically or horizontally from the floor plans

likewise, building sections should relate either vertically or horizontally to the floor plans or the building
elevations

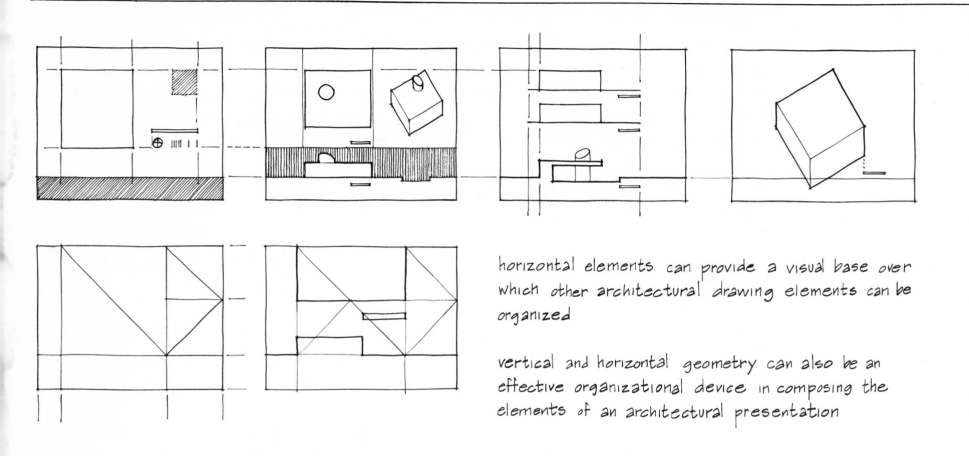

horizontal elements can provide a visual base over which other architectural drawing elements can be organized

vertical and horizontal geometry can also be an effective organizational device in composing the elements of an architectural presentation

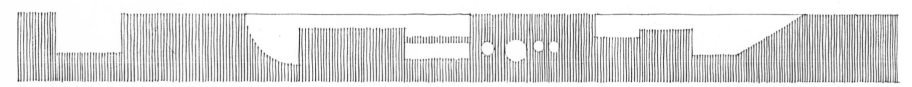

horizontal bands of some value can aid in reconciling dissimilar and irregular shapes and in reinforcing horizontal continuity

In conclusion, remember that drawing skills allow you to be eloquent, but you must first master the fundamentals. It takes discipline to draw a line, construct a perspective, or cast a shadow. It is hoped that this introduction to the basic elements of architectural graphics will provide you with a foundation upon which to build and develop the necessary physical and mental skills to communicate graphically with clarity and honesty.

"Art does not reproduce the visible; it renders visible" Paul Klee

INDEX